How to Love the Job You Hate

Also by Jane Boucher

The Assertive Communication Workbook
(CareerTrack)

The Body-Mind Connection
(Boucher Publishing)

How to Love the Job You Hate
(Thomas Nelson, Co. Publishers; Audio Edition: Padgett-Thompson)

Contributed to:
*Ordinary Women...Extraordinary Success: Everything You Need to Excel, from America's
Top Women Motivators* (Career Press)

Star Spangled Speakers (Royal Books)

Sound Selling...Do's and Don'ts for Boosting Self Esteem
(Audio: Nightingale Conant).

How to Love the Job You Hate
Job Satisfaction for the 21st Century

Jane Boucher, CSP

Reno, Nevada

How to Love the Job You Hate

Beagle Bay Books,
a division of Beagle Bay, Inc.
Reno, Nevada
info@beaglebay.com
Visit our website at: http://www.beaglebay.com

Book design: Robin P. Simonds
Editing: Robert Spear, Jacqueline Church Simonds

Library of Congress Cataloging-in-Publication Data

Boucher, Jane.
  How to love the job you hate : job satisfaction for the 21st century /
by Jane Boucher.
      p. cm.
A revision of the 1994 ed., which had no subtitle.
Includes bibliographical references and index.
  ISBN 0-9679591-0-1 (Trade paperback : alk. paper)
  1. Job satisfaction. 2. Self-esteem. 3. Job stress. 4. Stress
management. I. Title.

HF5549.5.J63B68 2004
650.1'3--dc22

                                                    2003023163

Printed in the United States

11 10 09 08 07 06 05 04   1 2 3 4 5

To my mother, Virginia Lee, who taught me the art of traveling to the beat of a different drummer

and

To my dad, Roy Boucher, who always traveled to the beat of that different drummer.

They taught me never to take "No" for an answer and to embrace life's challenges for all they are worth.

Work is love made visible . . .
And what is it to work with love?
It is to build the sandals as if your beloved were to wear them.
It is to crush the grapes as if your beloved were to drink the wine . . .
It is to charge all things you fashion with a breath of your own spirit.

—Kahlil Gibran

CONTENTS

FOREWORD XIII

ACKNOWLEDGMENTS XV

HOW TO LOVE THE JOB YOU HATE

CHAPTER ONE HOW TO LOVE THE JOB YOU HATE 3
    You Can Work Toward Greater Job Satisfaction 6

CHAPTER TWO HOW TO FALL IN LOVE AGAIN WITH YOUR JOB 8
    Twelve Ways to Put Spark In Your Work Life 10

CHAPTER THREE HOW TO LOVE THE PERSONALITY YOU HATE 25
    The Personality Types 26
    The Romantic Angle 30
    Flexibility and Acceptance Mean Emotional Maturity 30
    Working Against Your Personality Type 31
    Are You Masking Your True Personality? 32
    The Test You Cannot Fail 33

CHAPTER FOUR HOW TO LOVE THE BOSS YOU HATE 36
    Techniques of Good Management 38
    Manage Your Boss for a Change 42
    Understand Your Boss's Temperament 44

CHAPTER FIVE HOW TO LOVE THE CO-WORKER YOU HATE 48
    Communicate 49
    Listen 50
    Try a Little Respect 51
    Examine Your Contribution to Negative Relationships 51
    Recognize Your Differences 52
    Give Up the Need for Control 52
    Some Other Points to Consider 53
    On a Positive Note 55

CHAPTER SIX HOW TO LOVE THE COMPANY YOU HATE 58

Structure: Too Big, Too Small or Just Right? 59

Creating Job Satisfaction in a Small Company 60

Culture: Too Political, Too Conservative or Comfortable 63

Coping with the Company's Culture 64

Ethics: A Sticky Subject 67

CHAPTER SEVEN HOW TO LOVE YOURSELF 70

Techniques for Building Self-esteem 72

Is Work Your Source of Identity? 73

Recognizing Low Self-Esteem in the Workplace 74

First Aid for Self-esteem 76

What Is "Reaching Your Potential?" 80

CHAPTER EIGHT HOW TO LOVE THE STRESS YOU HATE 82

Why Are We So Vulnerable to Stress Today? 83

Recognizing the Need for Stress Management 83

Different Personality Types Can Handle Different Stress Levels . . . 86

How You Can Cope with Your Stress Level—Physically 87

How You Can Cope with Your Stress Level—Mental and Emotional
Effects 89

Stress and Company Culture 91

What Happens When Mental or Emotional Stress is Not Properly
Managed? 92

Are You At-Risk for Burnout or Depression? 93

First Aid for Stress 94

CHAPTER NINE HOW TO LOVE THE CRITICISM YOU HATE 99

The Give and Take of Criticism 100

Your Response 102

Anger: The Misunderstood Emotion 103

CHAPTER TEN LEAVING THE JOB YOU HATE 109

Analyze Your Current Job 110

Evaluating Your Options 112

Reasons to Quit a Job: the New Employer's Point of View 114

How Not to Quit Your Job 116

How to Leave Your Job Positively 117

Leaving your Job to Start Your Own Business 117

The Option for Kenny 118

CHAPTER ELEVEN LOSING THE JOB YOU LOVE 121

Coping Strategies 122

New Job Strategies 125

If You Are Facing A Lay-off 128

Think and Talk about Your Options. 129

SPECIAL SECTION FOR EMPLOYERS

CHAPTER TWELVE HOW TO LOVE THE EMPLOYEE YOU HATE 132

The Generation Gap and the Changing Employee 134

Behavioral Disabilities 135

The Personality Clash 136

There's Always One Rotten Apple 137

Handling the Problem Employee 139

CHAPTER THIRTEEN ADDRESSING YOUR EMPLOYEES' NEEDS 141

Stress 141

Mental Illness and Addictions 142

Self-Esteem 144

Domestic Violence Is a Workplace Issue 144

Physical Disabilities 146

Literacy and Basic Skills 147

Working with Your Employees 147

CHAPTER FOURTEEN PERFORMANCE EVALUATIONS WE ALL HATE 152

Creating the Right Tone for Communication 153

A Look at Various Appraisal Systems 154

Clarifying Expectations 156

Reviewing Accomplishments 158

Planning for Future Performance and Development 159

The Interpersonal Touch 160

When Evaluations Don't Go Well 160

The Value of Performance Evaluations 161

CHAPTER FIFTEEN MOTIVATING EMPLOYEES TO LOVE THEIR JOBS 163

Maximize Employee Potential, or "Potentialize" 165

Other Ways to Boost Motivation 169

Keeping the Motivator Motivated 169

CHAPTER SIXTEEN THE WHEEL OF LIFE: BALANCE IN AN UNBALANCED WORLD 172

The Wheel of Life: How the Spokes Support the Rim 172

A Final Word 181

SUGGESTED READING 183

ABOUT THE AUTHOR 185

INDEX 187

FOREWORD

Don't let that title fool you! It matters not whether you do indeed hate the job you have, or find yourself in a work situation that doesn't even begin to acknowledge or utilize all your talents, this book is for you! As you page through these chapters, you'll soon discover you're holding in your hands a compendium of proven and tested ideas that will make either situation a bit more tolerable.

Whether it be an uncomfortable partnership with your co-workers, a less than satisfactory relationship with your superiors, or even a company or organization that will never make anyone's "top ten zillion" best companies list, this book will give you the tools, tactics and techniques to help in any type of work situation. But before you start the celebration, there's work to be done. And that work starts with you!

Even with the ever-increasing use of technology on the job, we're still a "people business" society. You'll see Jane Boucher's expertise in this area of interpersonal relationships evidenced on every page. By exploring the different personality styles we all deal with on a daily basis, you'll discover the secrets to more harmonious working relationships.

Jane will take you on a journey that translates the latest research in the workplace and, by using real-world examples of real-world people in everyday situations we can all relate to, you'll soon learn that even the most negative situations still have that proverbial "silver lining."

However, you'll never find it without some soul-searching of your own.

So, if you really want to "take this job and shove it," make sure you first take the advice in this book and you may even find that you'll want to "take this job and love it!"

Edward E. Scannell, CMP, CSP
Past President, National Speakers' Association
Co-Author, *Games Trainers Play* series, McGraw-Hill.

ACKNOWLEDGMENTS

This book has been a dream come true. For many years, I've had a deep concern for American workers and their level of happiness on the job. We expend most of our energy during our workday, and our families get what's left. What happens to us at work affects every other area of our lives. It is my hope that as you read this book, you will learn how to find personal satisfaction in your job. *How to Love the Job You Hate* offers you practical tools to help you achieve greater peace of mind on the job.

I could not have written this book without inspiration. I thank God for my ability to write. I thank my parents Roy Boucher and Virginia Lee, for their continued encouragement and belief in my projects.

But the ideas have to take form. Geoffrey R. Lorenz, president and CEO of the Lorenz Corporation, took my idea, believed in it, and transformed it into a reality.

I am grateful to Sherry Money for her creative input and research Any endeavor is greatly enhanced when several minds come together toward a common goal. Sherry, I couldn't have done this book without you!

Many others have been instrumental in the development of this project. My deep appreciation goes to Don Thoren who provided constructive feedback for this revision. His support and help have been invaluable. I'm proud to call him my friend.

I thank Ed Scannell CMP, CSP, Director, Center for Professional Development, author of *Games Trainers Play* and other fine titles, for his words of wisdom. He has been a guiding light for anyone in the training business for over twenty years.

Many thanks go to Charlie "Tremendous" Jones, author of *Life is Tremendous*, for his belief in this project.

I'm grateful to Dr. Ken Blanchard, Chief Spiritual Officer of the Ken Blanchard companies, author of *The One Minute Manager*™ and other wonderful books, for taking the time to review this manuscript and to offer his full-fledged endorsement.

My sincere gratitude goes to my friend Nido Qubein, Chairman of the Great Harvest Bread Company, who also reviewed the manuscript. He offered invaluable insight and advice.

I am deeply grateful to my clients who have allowed me to grow with their organizations. Many of the stories in this book come from my experiences with them.

Dr. Jane Britt's sense of humor and common sense approach has gotten me through my toughest days. I have a profound sense of gratitude for her wise words.

I also want to thank my new publishers, Beagle Bay Books who had the vision to see the importance of this work. This revised version of my book, first published in Tennessee by Thomas Nelson, Inc., has become even more relevant today.

HOW TO LOVE THE JOB YOU HATE

"I've had one great passion in my life—hating my job."

CHAPTER ONE

HOW TO LOVE THE JOB YOU HATE

The United States is the only country in the world that has an unofficial end-of-the-work-week motto: Thank God it's Friday (TGIF). No matter how much you love what you do, the people you work with, or the challenges you face, there will always be days when you want to scream, "I hate this job!" If you find yourself saying this a little too often, this book can help.

My career as a professional speaker requires traveling around the U.S. offering seminars on job satisfaction and strategies on how to be successful in our employment relationships. I've found the time I spend talking to seminar attendees both valuable and illuminating. It's clear most people really want to do a good job and want their work to be both productive and satisfying. But when I ask seminar attendees if they feel satisfied with their time spent at work, the majority answer in the negative.

Learning how to love your work will bring a healthy, less stressful outlook, which can flow to other areas of your life. Increasing your happiness and fulfillment on the job can allow you to be better at it. In this new economy, your obvious satisfaction with your work will also help to make you much more competitive.

Why is this such a big deal? We spend too much time on the job not to care about it. In fact, we spend our "highest energy hours" working. Our families get what is left at the end of the day. Take a minute to add up the hours you devote, in some way, to your job each week. Start with a minimum of eight hours work, plus your commute, any planning time or work you bring home, plus the socialization or recreation activities associated with your job, such as a company softball team, bowling team or book club. Up to 80 percent of your waking hours are spent with work or co-workers.

In today's economy, where downsizing, mergers, buyouts, overseas outsourcing and business closings are rampant, changing jobs is not a practical solution to unhappiness with your boss or your job responsibilities. This is especially true if you have made some sort of emotional investment in your employment. Our jobs are very important, but we need to remember: *we are not our work*. Our jobs are meant to be the vehicle by which we get to where we want to be. They provide us our chosen lifestyle.

How to Love the Job You Hate offers strategies on how to look at your job in a different and more positive light. It is intended to be a how-to-guide. Though most of the chapters are written for an employee, there is also a special section that speaks directly to employers or people who supervise others. However, you should read the entire book. It applies to everyone who works, because employees and employers are all part of the same team.

Here are four stories that illustrate some common problems. Keep them in mind, as we'll revisit them throughout the book.

Ann is a forty-something program analyst for a government training facility. She has been in her job now for ten years. Almost seven years ago, she was assigned to take a course on terrorism in another city. She jumped at the chance, trying to grow in her skill-sets. When she returned, the duties of terrorism specialist (almost an afterthought, several years ago) were added to her job description. She has worked her way up the civil service ladder from the bottom and has been grateful for every promotion. As she advanced, she added her anti-terrorism duties to each new position.

Today Ann is angry that she must now compete with several others to win a newly created job as a Homeland Security Specialist. She feels she has earned respect in her workplace, driving over sixty-five miles—one-way—to work and she refuses to stay home sick, even when she has migraine headaches, which are now increasing in frequency. Although no other employee has any anti-terrorism experience, she must compete for the job because seven others senior to Ann have applied for the position. Two of her supervisors are among the applicants for the job, so Ann can expect no advocacy.

Uncharacteristically, Ann recently reminded a sympathetic co-worker that she never took a sick day off, even when she had migraines. She joked that if she woke up Monday morning with so much as a hangnail, she was going to rejoice and call in sick. Why? Because she feels she has been taken for granted at work, not just by her co-workers, but by her supervisors, as well.

Mark has been working for a luxury resort on the North Shore of Oahu for seven years. His job allows him to work flexible hours. His salary pays for his MBA, which he will finish this coming May. He has fun in the sun, meets a lot of people, shares a big beach house with several other students and makes great tips. His stress-relievers are surfing, hiking and girls he meets on his job as a bartender. He has been with the company long enough to be vested for full retirement when he is sixty. He's earned company privileges to stay in resorts all over the world.

Mark is dreading his coming graduation because it means he must make a decision that he has been avoiding. Company management likes him and has offered him a job in accounting, upon getting his degree. It's a generous proposition, but it comes with some loss of life-style flexibility. That and the high cost of living in Honolulu make him uneasy.

But does he really want to start over at a new company, with no benefits and lower wages? A junior accountant in another company wouldn't have Mark's current income. Yet, he always dreamed of moving back to the Midwest and climbing the corporate ladder to become a comptroller for a major firm.

Recently, he brought his parents and younger sister to Hawaii on what he saved in tips over the past year. The general manager put his family in a small suite as a gift from the resort's management. Mark feels that the "gift" is actually a very generous reminder that he is expected to take the position in the accounting department.

Mark has never discussed his plans with the general manager. He is at the point where he is not sure what he wants. He doesn't know if any of this matters, and he has begun to think he hates all of his job options.

Carole is an office manager for a large trucking company. She takes care of the business accounts, scheduling, payroll, business taxes and keeping the company current with government regulations and licenses. Carole is more aware than most company employees that a new series of regulations for the trucking industry will be very expensive for the company to follow. She has routinely been invited to all company business strategy sessions on critical issues. But something changed in the last few weeks, and she has not been included. She can't understand why her boss doesn't want her at those meetings anymore. She is terrified this may mean the company will close or they may be considering outsourcing her position as part of a cost-saving measure.

Leah, Carole's clerk, is cheerful and eager to please. Her work is consistently correct and completed on time. Lately, she has been sensing Carole's unease. She is frightened about taking time off for maternity leave. Leah looks to Carole for reassurance about her job and is not getting it.

Once Carole and Leah enjoyed an easy-going relationship. Now they keep their conversations to work-related topics. The tension between them grows daily.

Kenny, a thirty-year-old computer programmer, flies across the country two to three times a week unraveling computer problems for his company's clients. When he first took the job, he was a young single guy and the travel was exciting; he even goes to Hawaii a couple of times a year. But after three years of constant travel, as well as having moved his wife and small son three times to different parts of the country, he is not as happy anymore. He receives an excellent salary and incredible benefits, but he's overweight, gets no exercise, suffers from jet lag most of the time and rarely sees his wife who must cope with the moves to new communities virtually alone. Kenny's fears of becoming a stranger to his young son are beginning to undermine his love for his job.

Do any of these problems sound like you or someone you know?

You Can Work Toward Greater Job Satisfaction

This book has been written to help you in those areas of importance that you have some power to change. Though you may not have much control over your health insurance, benefits, or job security, you can have a definite and positive effect on:

- Making and keeping your work interesting
- Finding opportunities to learn new skills
- Being able to work independently
- Gaining recognition from co-workers
- Helping others in your job
- Limiting job stress and its effects
- Eliminating unnecessary overtime hours
- Seeing your work as important to society
- Enhancing your chances for promotion
- Increasing your contact with a lot of people

Actually, improving those areas helps make your job more secure in the current economic situation, because achieving greater satisfaction makes you a happier, more productive worker. In turn, you become a more valuable employee and less likely to be sacrificed when cuts are forthcoming. Learning to enhance your job satisfaction can even help you survive a job loss and make a smoother transition to a new position.

In the pages ahead, you will find ways of coping with the job you have, even if it, your boss or your co-workers are currently making you think you hate it. Try the practical suggestions I offer. See if you can turn TGIF into TGIM (Thank God It's Monday). You might even find yourself saying, "I love this job!"

CHAPTER TWO

HOW TO FALL IN LOVE AGAIN WITH YOUR JOB

George Burns, upon reaching his ninety-fifth birthday, was asked the secret of his longevity. He reportedly said one should fall in love with what one does. Note he didn't say, "Love what you do," or, "Do what you love," but rather, "Fall in love with what you do." That implies an active process. Try regarding your relationship with your job as much like a relationship with a person.

How do you fall in love with your job? Let's look at how you fall in love with a person. Granted, there is a sort of mystical quality about that special process. Most people think it happens by magic. But if you analyze it, you'll find there are some things that always happen when people fall in love.

Think about someone you love. That person isn't perfect, but you tend to concentrate on the things you love in him or her and minimize the weaknesses. If someone criticizes that person, you're likely to come up with all sorts of ways to excuse any failings brought to your attention. In fact, if the criticism is particularly severe, you might even get extreme in your defense of the loved one.

When was the last time you defended your job to that extent? Do you still concentrate on the things you like about your job? Or have you slipped into a "pity party," bemoaning all the things that annoy you about your job? Be honest with yourself. Are you giving too much weight to the things you don't like? Why didn't they bother you when you first started the job? Perhaps it was because you were still caught up in the excitement of the things you *did* like. Now it has become familiar. It's not new anymore. So, what do you do? Start concentrating on the good things again. Remind yourself of all the things you love about your work. In this, it is actually very much like love for a person. You must work on a relationship to keep it alive and growing. You can never ignore it and expect your relationship to continue to grow.

Remember that cliché about the seven-year-itch? That's the idea that even in the most loving marriage, after seven years, as a couple deals with all the vicissitudes of being married, things begin to go stale. Neither person believes the marriage is over or that there is less love, but the initial glow has gone. Part of the reason is these marital partners have been taking each other for granted. Over time, the initial excitement of the marriage wears off. Perhaps you both work and have routines at home where there are chores you two have divided up. You come home from work and, almost like robots, fall into those routines until you crawl into bed, exhausted. The seven-year-itch phenomenon is caused when one or both people in the marriage start looking outward for that "in love" feeling again. It's actually a good time to build something new into the relationship. After all, you have a seven-year emotional investment in that relationship. You need to stop and take the time to think of all the good things you love and appreciate about that person.

Just as in relationships, your job should be a reflection of the time you have been with the company. From that initial excitement you felt when you got the job you wanted—they picked you from all who applied for the job!—you've had years of growing, working with others who have become friends, tallying up the accomplishments for you and your company. Is it possible that you have come to a seven-year-itch with your job?

Something has happened to your attitude. Your familiarity has caused you to understand your job differently than when you first began. Now you know about problems and people and boring routines and annoying rules that you didn't know about when you applied for the job. No employment announcement will include the bad things. Again, it's very similar to being in love and finding that person's hair all over the sink or learning your love falls asleep right after dinner. Now that you understand these things and decide you're still in love anyway, you have to find a way to cope with those annoyances. You have to work on bringing the good things and the excitement back to the forefront.

In order to fall in love with what you do, you have to initiate the change. You need to know what you can do *specifically* each day to help you fall in love with what you do. Here are twelve suggestions that will help you change your attitude and put the spark back into your work life.

Twelve Ways to Put Spark In Your Work Life

1. Do Something Different

When you arrive at work, you probably have an established routine you follow. Maybe you devised it yourself or maybe it was imposed on you. The trick is to vary your schedule. Do something different from what you've done before. It may sound deceptively simple, but it can change your whole perspective. It's easy to become bored and apathetic about your workday when you're tied to one set pattern. "Same-old, same-old" can even get to the most precise and regulated person.

Try changing things around as much as you can. See if you can come up with a more interesting way to schedule your duties. If you have a routine meeting held at the same time every week, change the time or cancel it for a week. Your co-workers will probably appreciate the variation in routine, too.

If your lunch hour or breaks are flexible, move them around and have them at different times whenever you can. You might find that working while everyone else is at lunch, then having your meal when they get back, gives you some quiet time to concentrate.

Lunchtime can be the perfect hour to let off steam and refresh yourself for the rest of the day. Leave your workplace. The change in environment will do you good. If there is a nice outdoor spot near work, a wooded area or park, take your lunch there. Sitting in the fresh air and sunshine, even on a cool day, will have an amazingly rejuvenating impact on your attitude the rest of the day. In several cities, downtown businesses have banded together to offer seasonal noontime events such as live music and children's performances, outdoor brown-bag town meetings or farmer's markets. Lunchtime can have a relaxing, community flavor. Check your paper for events.

Make your lunch a "creative" break. Take a walk or read a book. To get your mind off work and give yourself a cooling down period, read something that is not work-related, such as a novel that allows you to escape the real world for a while.

If you feel you need to focus more on your career, read a book or a trade journal that is work-related. You may find some new ideas to get you out of the rut in your job.

You may want to visit a museum or art gallery to stimulate your creative thinking. Browsing through a bookstore can also get the creative juices flowing. Listening to music can help you relax.

Doing aerobics is good for your mental and physical health. There may be clubs or fitness centers you can join so that you can get into a structured class, work with a personal trainer, use sports equipment, eat a healthy lunch and even shower and change to return to work, refreshed.

The idea is to do something different, something to break the routine, relieve stress and stimulate your imagination. If you have too little time off for lunch to make these ideas work for you, bring it up to your employer as a suggestion, especially if you can show that it benefits the company beyond employee morale. Many employers really want to make their employees happier in their work and will do whatever they can afford to do.

For your part, it may be worth your while to negotiate flex-time hours and give yourself a longer break in the middle of the day. While your daily routine might be to eat a snack at your desk and get back to work so you can leave for home sooner, you should examine that. If you can possibly be at work earlier or stay later, changing your routine may be a solution for you. Flex-time allows workers to avoid the heaviest commuter traffic. Many large cities and municipalities welcome staggered work hours to help ease traffic congestion.

An important thing to realize in your work routine is that not every day will be one of excitement and rewarding fulfillment. Don't view the "off" days as boring. Use them as an opportunity to wind down with routine, "no-brain" activities. Then you can look forward to the days when more exciting things are happening.

For example, Joyce, a market researcher, thoroughly enjoys analyzing research data and turning the results into appropriate strategies to solve her client's marketing problems. But that is also the most challenging part of her job. It requires her most intense thinking and concentration. Though she loves it, if she had to do that constantly for eight hours every day, she would be mentally exhausted all the time. Therefore, Joyce appreciates the simple tasks of sorting surveys and tabulating data that come first in the process. The variety lets her wind down between strategy sessions, so she can be fresh for the more exciting and creative part of her job.

Don't put off doing the things you dislike. It's better to put them first on your "to do" list so you can get them out of the way and go on to things you enjoy. You might even want to come in a little early or stay a little later to get boring work done and off your mind. If you are a person who likes to put off the less pleasant things, remember that once they are done, they are out of the way. If you do the pleasant things first, the unpleasant ones are in the back of your mind all day, reminding you that the worst is yet to come. Getting those more unpleasant items out of the way will leave your favorite things to do seem like a reward.

2. Delegate the Things You Don't Like to Do

Think of the tasks in your job you really don't like to do. I'm not suggesting jobs that are necessary as a part of a process, but the kinds of things that you hate doing and that someone else may actually like to do. Perhaps your co-worker wouldn't mind making telephone calls for you, if you would do some paperwork for them. An exchange of tasks like that can help relieve boredom and stress for both of you, as well as strengthening your working relationships.

If there are responsibilities in your job description that you believe are not appropriate for your job, and you have to stay late frequently to complete them, you have two options: work out an exchange or change the way you view the tasks. You may find another employee who wants to do your assignments in exchange for something you can do for them. The two of you should then sit down with your supervisor. Or you can find a new way of looking at the duties (See Number One "Do Something Different").

You may have an assistant or subordinate who would appreciate the chance to take on a new responsibility. This can also help the other person in their professional growth. They will bring their own creative style to a task that feels mundane to you. The only caution for this particular situation is you must carefully monitor that person, prior to setting them free to do the work, especially if it involves interacting with the public.

Cross-training is healthy for both employee and employer as it enables a person to try different tasks. Make sure you run this sort of exchange by your supervisor, so that the subordinate always gets credit for this new skill-set.

That brings us to my second caution. Whatever it is that you don't like to do, it is probably still an important task. We tend to belittle tasks we dislike. Just make sure that, no matter how small, the work is completed on time, responsibly. Also, make sure the exchanges are equitable. Delegating additional duties to a subordinate is tricky and can be unfair unless you offer to take some tasks off their shoulders.

3. Avoid Complaining

There are people in every organization who will always have something negative to say, without offering any possible solutions. You're probably familiar with the type. No matter what happens on the job, even if the situation seems positive to everyone else, these people manage to find something negative to say about it. When the boss announces a raise for everyone, starting next month, these folks will inevitably complain that it should have happened last month.

You should recognize the difference between constructive criticism—designed to find a solution to a problem—and chronic complaining. Be careful not to label someone a complainer when they are simply analytical people who can foresee potential difficulties. Remember that someone in the organization needs to present that point of view. Of course, it should not become the routine response to every project or suggestion. The person who seems to be unyieldingly negative without being flexible enough to accept solution or compromise, can be a drain on morale.

The best thing to do with people like that is to avoid getting too involved with them. However, if your boss, an important client, or a co-worker is one of the chronic complainers, that's not always possible. In that case, be as cooperative as you can, but mentally separate that person's attitude from yours.

Perhaps that person is having a tough time. A kind word and your understanding attitude can help your relationship and even help you. Saying, "I realize you have a lot to deal with right now, but I think you're handling it really well," can help diffuse the anger of a person who is ready to launch into a complaint session.

A tactful way to steer clear of listening to gripes about a third party is to say, "I know things have been difficult, but I'll be glad to help you get some of that extra work done." Thus you acknowledge that the complainer is experiencing a problem without getting too involved. It never helps to take sides with one person against another when you are not concerned in the situation. You probably have to work with both people, so you should stay as neutral as you can. By offering your help with a specific task you offer a solution that will make the complainer feel better, but aren't adding fuel to his or her anger.

Perhaps you are a person who feels sharing your opinion is not complaining. Try to understand not everyone feels as you do. Be sensitive to your co-worker's reactions. Some may find your expressions stressful. Others who are worried about their job may feel that to be caught listening to criticism of the company could endanger their further employment. In some cases, you may be undermining your own good intentions.

4. Build Good Working Relationships with Your Co-workers

Few things can make your work life more unpleasant than difficult co-workers. One young woman was ready to quit her job because of problems she perceived with her co-workers. Lynn thought her workplace was full of cliques. She knew that every time she went on break or to lunch, the others talked about her. She thought they didn't like her because she did her job well, observed proper break periods, came to work on time every day and so on. But was she actually the topic of department conversation? Had she ever approached her boss and explained her feelings? Had she ever approached any of her co-workers and asked them to go to lunch or to have a private talk to discuss her feelings? No, she simply "knew." On a couple of occasions, she had even tried to transfer to another department. Because she was doing a good job where she was, her boss was reluctant to let her go.

Lynn finally realized she had to talk to someone about the situation. It had caused her undue stress for nearly two years. When she discussed it with her boss, it turned out that he was unaware of her feelings, but understood and provided some significant feedback. He suggested a number of co-workers to whom she could talk about her feelings. In a few days it became apparent to Lynn that only a small portion of her complaint was valid. Much of the tension was created by her tone of voice, body language and subconscious defensive reactions toward others. The point of this illustration is that many people imagine they have problems with co-workers, yet they have never really taken the time to communicate with people or make an effort to build good relationships. You probably spend more waking time with your co-workers than you do with your family and friends. It is only logical that such important relationships require at least as much effort as you give to your friendships.

Do you have a relationship at work that is particularly difficult? Most likely, it can be repaired. Go to the person and ask him or her sincerely, "What can I do to help us work together more effectively?" Note the emphasis on *I*, not you or we. Even if the other person is the cause, your effort to change the relationship without finding fault can soften the person and maybe even encourage them to open up and admit his faults too. Nine times out of ten, this approach will work. When it doesn't, don't let that other person's negative attitude affect your own. If you have made the honest effort to work things out and he refuses, it's not your fault. But if a difficult relationship can be improved, you will feel a lot better about going to work every day.

Another way to build good co-worker relationships is to initiate some get-togethers, such as going to lunch or going out to unwind together after work. That can be a good way to get to know people better and develop support for each other. You can even share concerns and look for ways to solve work-related problems. Be careful not to let it turn into a gossip circle or a clique that excludes certain people, however. Slinging mud will only cause you to lose ground.

Starting a support group, an exercise class, diet group or sports teams are all effective ways to build camaraderie and create team spirit. You might point out to management that a basketball hoop, a VCR or DVD for the lounge or a picnic table is an investment in employee satisfaction that certainly costs less than dealing with stress-related illnesses or even replacing people. Those are good ways to include people from other departments as well. Getting to know people you don't normally associate with can help you learn more about the company and make contacts that could be valuable to your career in the future.

For more ways of coping with co-workers, you'll find extensive suggestions in Chapter Six: *How to Love the Co-Worker You Hate*.

5. Build a Good Relationship with Your Boss

Many work-related complaints are directed at bosses. The nature of the relationship between worker and boss automatically causes friction. After all, it means one person tells another person what to do. That is why supervisors need a great deal of skill in handling people, as well as a thorough knowledge of their job. If you have a boss who is deficient in either of those areas, you are going to have problems. As a worker, you also need to understand the pressure and responsibility your supervisor faces and the stress that causes. Remember that there are two sides to every story.

The key to building a good relationship with your boss is opening the lines of communication and keeping them open. As with your co-workers, you may have to initiate this process. Many people are afraid to approach their boss for fear of losing their job, but your attitude can make it work for both of you. It is better to confront problems in the relationship than to try to avoid them. They will not get better by themselves. Ask your boss for a meeting at his or her convenience. Tell your supervisor you want to talk about ways to do your job better. Don't set a meeting when you are angry or upset. Wait until you feel you are in control of your emotions. Then, offer suggestions and ask for feedback. Don't make demands or place blame. Don't speak in terms of emotions, feelings or assumptions you may have.

Your boss may be under a tremendous amount of stress and not aware that there is a problem. The other possibility is that your boss is actually frightened of coming across in the wrong way. He or she is trying so hard to be objective, fair and "all business" that they may not know how to solve the problem without seeming to look weak or foolish

The technique suggested under Number Three "Avoid Complaining", to approach a co-worker by quietly asking, "How can I do a better job, or work in a way that you would find more satisfactory?" is again, a good idea. It is not disrespectful nor does it place blame. It opens the lines of communication and allows your boss to talk frankly with you. You should be prepared to hear what your boss says—good or bad. He or she may be relieved to have the opportunity to address the situation and appreciate you for that. You are showing trust.

Your relationship with your boss is such an important part of your work life and job satisfaction that Chapter Five: *How to Love the Boss You Hate* is devoted to this subject.

6. Create Your Own Special Project

This is a great way to feel excited about your job and fall in love all over again. Working on a special project that is all yours can help give you a sense of control and contribution. There are many ways to initiate this. Ask your boss what needs to be done, or enlist his or her support for an idea of your own that can benefit both you and the company. You might propose a new approach to an old problem. You could be aware of a way to save the company money. You deal with things daily that may not be as efficient as they could be, or procedures that are outdated, duplicated or wasteful. Your boss might not notice these things, but because you work closely with them, you can bring them to his or her attention and make both of you look good.

Be creative and inventive, but above all, be assertive in going for this project. Assertive does not mean aggressive, which is overbearing, pushy or demanding. Speak up when you have an idea and follow it through with well-thought-out reasoning and support. Ask your co-workers about your proposal to find out how much others would support the change. Be prepared to explain that it won't create more problems for anyone other than you. Don't be offended if co-workers are afraid of change or think it may involve their having to learn new ways of doing things. If your idea is not exactly a money-saver, investigate a bit. Could it create a more positive cash flow for the department or the company? Any streamlining or even an idea that pleases customers and creates business satisfaction saves a company money, if indirectly.

Carefully examine the details and make sure the project is something in which you are willing to invest your time and energy. Once you have made a suggestion, or initiated a project, continue to promote it until you get a definite response.

Deborah was a telephone customer-assistant, working in the accounting department of a company that designed and installed home entertainment systems. The company grew more quickly than the owners had anticipated, so they added an automatic phone answering system. Customers used voice mail to reach the assistants or order new phases of their systems. Deborah noticed that every few days a customer would call her department wanting to update or add to their system. She would politely tell them that they had reached the wrong department and advised them to re-enter the voice mail menu. Deborah was a bit upset that she kept getting these calls by mistake. In a monthly staff meeting, the sales department reported that they had very few customers calling to update systems. Returning customer sales had been going so well and the feedback survey cards were always positive when the first components were installed in the homes. They couldn't figure out what had happened.

Deborah felt the little light-bulb go on in her head. When she got home she dialed the company number, listened to the automated menu and dialed as instructed. Instead of hearing instructions to leave a message to improve their systems, she was transferred to hold—where easy listening music played for eleven minutes before she was disconnected. Deborah was excited that she had solved the mystery, but realized that something would have to be done quickly to repair the poor business relations incurred by the mistake. She drew up a plan for sales people, detailing how they could convey their apologies by personal contact and a discount to existing customers. When Deborah got to work the next morning, she softened the blow of the terrible news by offering a plan to recoup the good will for the company.

Within two weeks, the manager got such good feedback from customers that Deborah was offered the newly created job of sales support specialist and a very nice raise. Deborah was even given a box of her new business cards—the first in her career.

Kelly was a top-notch salesperson in a small women's fashion store for five years. The store had an excellent reputation but was starting to lose sales to some of its larger competitors. Kelly suggested to the owner that they do a customer survey. The owner didn't see the need at first, but whenever problems occurred or it was noticed that certain customers weren't coming in anymore, Kelly pointed out how a survey would let them know what was wrong and what they could do differently.

The owner finally agreed. Kelly immediately produced the survey master copy that she'd developed. Once Kelly and her boss got the results, it was discovered that the store could easily fix its problems. The owner was quite impressed with Kelly's perceptiveness and understanding of the customer's needs. A few months later, when sales began picking up, Kelly was promoted to assistant manager and allowed to participate in the buying decisions.

If you run into resistance and your idea seems to cause more problems than it solves, accept that. Dwelling on the rejection of your idea can damage your performance and your self-esteem. Here is an important suggestion for a special project that is not used or accepted: keep a copy or a written record of the project for yourself. You put a lot of time into it, and you should never consider that a waste. By creating your first big project, you can include that in your portfolio as new experience and skills. It may even become an important contribution to your company or career in the future.

Remember that people will never know the great things you are capable of if you don't tell them. There may come a time later when it is obvious to your supervisor that your project is necessary and valuable to the company. Give it time and re-suggest it when the need for it arises.

7. Learn Something New

The quickest way to stop growing and begin falling out of love with your job is to stop learning. Expanding your knowledge or skills makes you feel like you are accomplishing more, which in turn makes you feel more successful. The joy of learning and discovery carries a tinge of romantic adventure that will give you a new reason to fall in love with your job. Is there a part of your job that you have always wanted to know more about? Perhaps you need some improvement in a specific area of your work. Why not take a class at a night school or local community college? You may even decide to begin work on an advanced degree in your field. Would you enjoy attending professional seminars or becoming involved with a professional organization? There are many good ways to expand your skills and reactivate a stagnant career path.

Perhaps your field has areas of specialization you would like to explore. College, technical or vocational school classes can help you do that, or a general career-planning course can help you clarify your career goals. Someone in your own company may be able to advise you on how to pursue a more specialized path or may be willing to teach you some new skills. All of those things will increase your knowledge of the organization, making you more valuable, opening doors for possible advancement in the future.

8. Get Involved in Your Company's Community Service Activities

There are all kinds of community service organizations and projects that could benefit from the support of your company or a group of people in your company. Why not initiate a company project? Find out how many other workers would be interested. This not only helps you and your fellow co-workers feel good about yourselves and your work; it can also generate excellent publicity for your company. What follows are just a few examples:

- Organize a committee to help plan fund-raising events in your company. Use the money collected throughout the year for a needy family during the holidays. There are a number of social service organizations that can match up your company with a family who needs your help.

- Plan a holiday party. It doesn't have to be at Christmas—in fact it might be better if it is not a religious holiday since everyone else is doing something then. Perhaps Labor Day or other holiday. Invite people in a nursing home or children in an economically deprived area. Hold the party at the office, or if that isn't practical, hold it at their building, school, public park or community center.

- You might want to "adopt" a particular class at a school—or the whole school. Hold special learning days, teaching them about what your company does and how they might plan for a future in your career field. Take them on a special field trip or out for a picnic on a Saturday. Each one of your co-workers could really make a difference in a child's life if your company were to help with schoolwork for an hour per week.

- Adults need help with life skills like budgeting, acquiring new job skills and, most importantly, literacy. In almost every area of interest a person has, local agencies have already set up programs with participants hoping for volunteers to show up.

- Have your company join Habitat for Humanity. President Jimmy Carter and his wife still pack hammers and work clothes to help build houses with Habit for Humanity every year. That agency and others have all the organizational plans and materials ready for your company to participate. Companies can join in these programs for just a day or weeks at a time.

- For just about every idea you can come up with, there are almost always programs in place to help you carry it out. For example, a successful homeless shelter program in San Diego works with visiting major corporations from all over the United States. The companies plan a retreat at the convention center, located right across the street from the shelter. As part of the program, they perform a building or cleaning project at the shelter program. A corporate liaison works with the shelter to prepare all year for the event. Smaller companies provide volunteers to serve meals for one week every year. This program is so successful that meal servers are booked for every day, a year in advance.

- Your company could form a cooperative educational effort with other businesses. Each company can contribute something to an overall program that enriches the lives of people in less fortunate circumstances. The possibilities are endless!

Begin by doing your homework. Figure out what would best suit your co-workers and your company. Discuss it with them. Ask your supervisor what your business would be interested in supporting. Consider the logistics of including everyone who would want to participate and make a plan you think the majority of your co-workers would support. It would be helpful to avoid religious or political organizations to be as inclusive as possible. Instead of volunteering your professional talents, maybe your co-workers would benefit from doing something completely different than their duties at work.

Your supervisors might want to start with something that actually benefits the company, just to get comfortable with the whole idea of community service. Open a few internship positions through your local community college and offer to supervise a college student who may, one day after graduation, be a future employee.

As an individual, you can volunteer your skills to a nonprofit organization. Are you an accountant? Help with records and bookkeeping. Are you in advertising or public relations? Offer to create effective fund-raising campaigns or public service, spot, radio and television commercials. Are you a teacher or a writer? Many underprivileged children and illiterate adults could benefit from your help in learning to read. You can find hundreds of ways to use your job skills creatively to help others, and make your work feel truly rewarding. This could not only help you fall in love with your job again; you might just fall in love with yourself because volunteering feels so good.

9. Rewrite Your Job Description

The tasks for each job should be documented. Perhaps there was never a job audit to tell the worker what tasks should be listed under each job description.

As an example, consider a telephone receptionist hired to work at a new small business. She didn't mind ordering office supplies when the phones weren't busy. Twenty years later, the present receptionist handles twelve telephone lines, in-person appointments, walk-ins and has to stay late twice a month to inventory office supplies. If the person is a conscientious worker, he or she will even find the best prices for various office supplies and make orders from different vendors. Then someone has to approve the expense so the order must be sent to accounting. Obviously this task has outgrown its place under the receptionist's job description.

It's no one's fault that the company grew larger and the two tasks grew too much for one person. At the same time, that original receptionist, wanting to grow with the company, should have been allowed to list her duties with the supplies as experience. If she liked that sort of task, she might have pursued that sort of career when training and entry-level positions became available.

Having employees write their own job descriptions is my favorite suggestion, because it can be a reward for the hard work for which they've not been given credit. Often it is the first time it has been done by the person actually in the position. The personnel office, supervisors or company owners may have written the original job descriptions thinking they knew all that the job entailed, but like everything else, employment positions change. Perhaps a worker has particular skills they brought to the job. These expand the job description in ways an employer couldn't have predicted. It is a safe bet that if an employee has been in the position for a lengthy amount of time, the job has evolved. Once these job descriptions are written, the personnel office or supervisor should take time to re-evaluate the position.

Have you learned everything you can about your job? Do you know how it fits into the big picture for your company? If you think you have mastered you job, try to learn about the jobs of people around you. You will find this can help you understand your own position better.

One day when things were slow for Dan, a direct mail copywriter, he was asked to help sort response cards returned by recipients of a mailing. Seeing how people filled out the response gave Dan invaluable insight into more effective ways to write and design the cards. That, of course, made him a better copywriter.

Rewrite your job description to include tasks you do best. Include all additional duties that you can handle in your boss or co-worker's absence. Write any new ideas, projects, or procedures that you have implemented, plus any new educational advancements you have made, related to the position. All this should help you to see yourself in a new light. You will see how far you've progressed since you started the job and how valuable you are to the company.

10. Create Your Own Personal Mission Statement

You may think you already have an idea of what you want to accomplish in your career. But it can be surprisingly helpful and enlightening to write it out. Mapping out a plan that puts all of your life goals into perspective can greatly affect your feelings about your present job. Here are some suggestions on how to write out a personal mission statement:

Write a brief description of the main goal in your life's work. Your faith or personal philosophy will have a great deal of influence on this. The statement can be very simple. For example, a nurse may write, "To be especially understanding and comforting to people who are ill and to help their loved ones cope." Even a store clerk or gas station attendant can take satisfaction in his or her work by striving "to be accurate in details and helpful to customers."

Now evaluate what you've written with these questions in mind:

- How does your job fit into this plan? Is it just to pay the bills or is this part of your "master plan."

- Does your current employment offer you an opportunity to fulfill your mission, or thwart it?

- Will your job enable you to develop strengths that will benefit you?

- Does this work allow you to work with a mentor or career advocate?

- Do they offer you the particular kind of experience from which you can learn?

All of these questions can help you determine whether you are on the track fulfilling your personal goals or whether you need to switch to a different track.

11. Give Yourself Credit for What You Accomplish

Keep a special "me" file in your desk that you can pull out and look at on days when things are going wrong or when you feel unappreciated. The file should contain any awards, certificates of commendation, college transcripts or notes of appreciation from supervisors, clients or co-workers. Even if someone compliments your work verbally, write yourself a little note about the conversation, date it and tuck it into that file. This is not being egotistical. Even if you are the only one to ever see this file, you deserve to be reminded of the good things you do.

Another entry in your "me" file should be an updated résumé. Even if you are not looking for another job, keep it up-to-date with your current accomplishments and skills. That will help you see how far you have come in your career development. Of course, it can also come in handy if you do come across an irresistible job opportunity.

Here is something else that can be invaluable in you "me" file—you might call it a "me résumé." It is a list of specific things at which you consider yourself an expert on your job. These are not the kind of things that normally go into a job description, but they become very much a part of the job for you. They are all the little things that count, such as knowing just what to say to a particularly difficult client. Perhaps you have developed a knack for writing up invoices so they get processed twice as fast. You may be the only person in your department who knows how to change the paper in the fax machine.

However small you may think those things are, they are immensely important to getting the job done. Give yourself credit. You deserve it.

12. The Myth of Batting 1000: Don't Give Up

You may try your best to make your job enjoyable, but there will always be things that cause you problems. Not everything you do will work, but does that mean you shouldn't try? Of course not. Did you know that in baseball, a batting average of .300—which means three hits out of ten times at bat—is considered great? Babe Ruth's career batting average was .342. That means he had an average of 3.42 hits out of ten times at bat. Remember that when you are disappointed with your job, with a co-worker, a boss or even yourself. Sometimes, it may seem less painful to say, "If they don't care, then why should I?" But in reality, you will feel better if you can say, "At least I care about my job, and I know I am trying my best." Say that to someone you can talk to and trust. Telling someone else who understands will at least help you feel like your effort was acknowledged. You can also gain satisfaction from encouraging your co-workers who might be suffering through a negative job situation with you.

These twelve suggestions are designed to help you rekindle a feeling of excitement and positive focus about your job. One thing you don't want to do is try to do all of them at once. Set realistic goals for yourself by studying them carefully and deciding which ones you can work on first. Don't overload yourself by taking on extra classes, extra projects, and community service work all at once. It is best to start one project and divide it in to manageable stages. Allow yourself to be successful at each stage, and let that encouragement motivate you further.

CHAPTER THREE

HOW TO LOVE THE PERSONALITY YOU HATE

At some time in your life, you have probably asked age-old questions that apply to all kinds of relationships: "Why doesn't that person think as I do?" You may have thought, "That person is just like so-and-so," or "That person is just like me." You undoubtedly recognize that there are obvious personality differences among people, but you may never have analyzed their patterns and how those differences affect relationships.

As far back as 400 B.C., Hippocrates, considered the father of medicine, analyzed four basic personality types, or temperaments. He based the four types on the predominance of certain body fluids: blood, yellow bile, black bile, and phlegm. He named them: sanguine (blood), choleric (yellow bile), melancholy (black bile), and phlegmatic (phlegm). Today, we know that personality types are not related to these fluids. But many psychologists do agree that the biochemical structure of the brain is related to the four personality types and combinations thereof.

There are numerous tests and systems now being used by psychologists and employers based on this four-type model. They use different names for them, but they are all based on the same information. For example, Performax Systems International, Inc. analyzes whether a person's behavioral tendency is Influence, Dominance, Compliance or Steadiness. Those are the equivalent of sanguine, choleric, melancholy and phlegmatic. The Merril-Reid Social Styles use the terms Expressive, Driving, Analytical, and Amiable in the same respective order.

I have developed a more descriptive set of types for use in my seminars. The following will give you a brief introduction to each. I have also included a more detailed test in this chapter, so you can determine your types. Most people are a combination. Some can even be a blend of three—usually with two of the three being more dominant. You may occasionally see aspects of each type in yourself, but I want you to think in terms of what best describes you the majority of the time. If you think all fit you equally, that may indicate that you feel some confusion about your personality. Perhaps you are not sure who your really are. We'll explain more about this later in the chapter.

The Personality Types

Are You a People-Person?

The people-person is Hippocrates' sanguine. The original name came from the word *blood*. Hippocrates thought these people had a predominance of blood as they were warm, friendly, outgoing and generally well-liked. People-persons love people, and others seem to gravitate naturally to them. They are especially known for their talkativeness and love to be entertaining. They like to encourage others to have fun. They are comfortable in a roomful of total strangers when they can talk to everyone around them, usually asking all sorts of questions and telling their own life story to anyone who will listen. They are particularly good at turning a mundane event into an exciting and colorful story, sometimes stretching the truth to its outermost limits—but all in the name of fun! For that reason they are usually excellent speakers and salespeople.

Because of their openness and warmth, people-persons are sought for help with problems of all kinds. They can find the bright side in almost any situation. They hate to say no, even if they want to, because they want everyone to like them. Because of that desire to please others, they often find themselves over-committed.

In terms of work, people-persons find their greatest satisfaction in people-oriented professions such as teaching, counseling, sales, public relations, acting, religious occupations, social work and healthcare. Paperwork and organizational procedures tend to frustrate them, as they would rather just deal with people.

To the other personality types, people-persons can appear to be tremendous egotists. In reality, this extroverted, action-oriented temperament needs to see a response to his or her actions. That means that all of their inner thoughts are almost instantly translated into outward action (especially verbally), sometimes resulting in foot-in-mouth syndrome. But people-persons really just need to feel appreciated. A compliment or a pat on the back often means more to them than high pay.

President Bill Clinton is a good example of a people-person. The former President's charismatic personality drew many people to him. He is well-known for staying up into the wee-hours discussing national policy with anyone who can stay awake. Like most people-persons, helping people—through his political agenda—gives him great satisfaction. In his case, the very personality temperament that resulted in his success caused him personal and political problems.

Are You a Command-Person?

The command-person is Hippocrates' choleric. He thought these people were full of hot, yellow bile because they often seemed to be angry and explosive. Command-persons are extroverted and action-oriented like people-persons, but they are usually more blunt. They are bottom-line, results-oriented people who want to accomplish their goals. Obstacles are seen as challenges to be overcome. Failure is rarely a part of the command-person's vocabulary, but even if it happens, he or she never quits—they just move on to the next project.

Command-persons are natural-born leaders, the decision-makers, the entrepreneurs and managers who make things happen. In other words, command-persons like to be in charge. That doesn't always mean they will be the boss, at least in the technical sense. Command-persons can be happy in subordinate positions, as long as they feel in charge of their own projects. They may also feel the need to give advice by occasionally telling co-workers how to do their work. This can lead co-workers, family and friends to complain that the command-person is aggressive, domineering and bossy.

At their best, however, command-persons are great motivators and inspiring leaders. They are happiest when they can fully utilize their abilities to accomplish a goal or complete a project, which they can do best when they are given the authority to direct the project themselves and delegate tasks. Achievement is their greatest satisfaction.

President George W. Bush is an example of a more dominant command-person. He knows what he wants and how he wants to get it done. He surrounds himself with trusted and experienced people who get the job done exactly the way he wants it. His command-person traits serve him well in his drive to fulfill his legislative agenda.

Are You a Detail-Person?

The detail-person, or Hippocrates' melancholy, is the one who wants to analyze and interpret information. Whereas people-persons and command-persons tend to be bored by minutiae, detail-persons want to know how things come together. Detail-persons are thinkers who like to dig into abstract ideas and theories. They are introverted people who tend to think long and hard about something before giving an answer or opinion. They must be provided with all the facts, figures, and details before making a decision. They may frustrate the people-persons or command-persons who tend to act quickly without putting a lot of thought into their decisions.

Detail-persons often become engineers, physicists, doctors, college teachers, economists, or computer systems analysts. But they may also choose less technical professions, such as writing or architecture. The key to the detail-person's satisfaction is being able to analyze. He or she needs to create new meanings and methods or improve existing methods and systems.

Detail-persons usually work well with minimal supervision and are frustrated with office politics, poor organization or systems that don't work. They may sometimes be perceived as loners because they are not strong in interactive people skills. That does not mean they don't like people, but they may seem cold and unresponsive because of their introverted nature.

Because detail-persons like to analyze things, they have a tendency to see all the negatives in a situation. That tendency may make the detail-person look like a complainer to the more positive people-persons and command-persons.

Albert Einstein was undoubtedly a detail-person. He was famous for analyzing facts, statistics, and data to discover new theorems, including the Theory of Relativity. But he was certainly not known for his people skills. In fact, he was a very shy man. Like all detail-persons, he was happiest poring over ideas and theories with the freedom and time to analyze them.

Are You a Support-Person?

Hippocrates' fourth type is the phlegmatic, or support-person. This is the person who works quietly in the corner, always seems to have a pleasant response, and never seems to let anything bother him or her. Support-persons are often taken for granted, but they provide the support structure that keeps an organization going. Support-persons generally prefer to work behind the scenes, as they are usually introverted, quiet people. They prefer established procedures and routines. They are usually patient and thorough, and often do the jobs that others may find boring. Fields such as bookkeeping, accounting, statistics, engineering, drafting, computers and skilled mechanical work are often enjoyed by support-persons. Because of their patient, diplomatic nature, they are also good at teaching and counseling.

Support-persons are usually reluctant leaders, but if put into a managerial position, they are good organizers and mediators. Support-persons generally dislike conflict, therefore, they are good at keeping things flowing in a harmonious fashion. They like to keep things orderly and predictable. One of their strengths is that they are the steadiest and most reliable of the temperaments. Support-persons are happiest when the environment is peaceful and without conflict. They gain genuine satisfaction from helping others achieve their goals.

Though not outgoing, support-persons usually have good people skills. They are rarely the initiators of a relationship or conversation, but once approached, they are friendly and particularly empathetic. Support-persons are excellent listeners. They often attract people who either need sympathy or like to talk, because the support-person will rarely be rude. Occasionally, when backed into a corner by a threatening person or situation, a support-person will snap at someone. That is usually a great surprise to the threatening person, because it is so rare. One of the support-person's greatest weaknesses is letting others take advantage of him or her.

Support-persons can be incredibly stubborn. They can dig in their heels and refuse to budge; though this tactic is very subtle. Instead of screaming or raging like a people-person, barking orders like a command-person, or refusing to speak like a detail-person, the angry support-person simply won't have your report typed when you want it finished. Or, if the support-person is an accountant, you won't get any of your expense checks until the problem is resolved.

Support-persons are also famous for their delightful, dry sense of humor. Comedian Jerry Seinfeld's character on his successful television show was a support-person. His seemingly thoughtful, dry reactions to the other characters on the show were timed so perfectly that one simple word of agreement (when he obviously did not agree) or just a questioning glance toward the camera would result in hysteria from the audience. The character was always the nice guy whose friends are constantly taking advantage of him or trying to enlist him in their self-serving antics. His calm, steady nature, his boyish grin and constant need to appear politically correct while avoiding the most justifiable confrontations appealed to an entire generation. He finds humor in his observations of life as a spectator, never as a participant.

The Romantic Angle

An interesting point about personality types is that, in romance, opposites tend to attract. In a work situation, you may work best with those who think like you. However, you may find that your choice of mate will be someone who isn't like you at all. Even close friends are often people of opposite temperaments. This seems to happen because you are attracted to something in another person that you perceive is missing in yourself.

Kim, a people-person, fell in love with Michael, a detail-person, because he could explain things in such detail that she understood exactly what he meant. She was fascinated by his careful way of analyzing life, as she had never thought of it before. Bill, a command-person, fell in love with Deirdre, a support-person, because she listened intently to all of his ideas about work projects. According to Bill, most other women got bored listening to him. An understanding of personality types also becomes a valuable marriage counseling tool when opposites begin to irritate each other.

Flexibility and Acceptance Mean Emotional Maturity

Einstein, a detail-person, was an analyzer and something of a loner. President George W. Bush, a command-person, is a decision-maker who delegates effectively. Bill Clinton's people-person skill propelled him into the White House and helped him achieve many of his goals while in office. Jerry Seinfield's TV persona, a support person, placates his friends to hilarious results. No one style is good or bad. Although the people-persons and command-persons may say, "Just do it!" and the detail-persons reply, "I'll have to think about it"—each style works well for the individual. Each temperament must be seen as adding a piece to the puzzle, creating a whole, balanced picture. Someone has to see the obstacles, and someone has to have the determination to overcome them. So, when the detail-person says, "Here's the problem," the people-person or command-person can say, "You're right. And here's how we can solve it."

The important thing to remember about the four personality types is that there are no strict, inflexible characterizations. Most people are a combination of two types. President John F. Kennedy was a command / people-person. During his short term in office, he accomplished a number of goals that had far-reaching effects on our nation and the world, including the space program, the Civil Rights bill, the Peace Corps and the prevention of a nuclear war. His strong command-person side blended with his accessible and likable people-person side to make him one of the most popular presidents in our history.

Even those who are predominantly one type can be flexible and adaptable enough to function in the role of other types when necessary. This ability is related to a person's emotional maturity and self-esteem. While this will be discussed in more detail in Chapter Eight: *How to Love Yourself*, you must remember that a personality type is, still and all, part of that bigger and forever changing picture.

Working Against Your Personality Type

Keep your personality type in mind when you evaluate your feelings about your job. If you are currently working and really hate it, perhaps it doesn't suit your temperament. Do not beat yourself up for hating a job that others may think is the greatest, most lucrative employment opportunity in the world. You are who you are and we all react to situations for different reasons. I can't imagine waking up tomorrow, finding out that I'm a rock star, and hating it. However, I don't know because I've never been one. The point is that when a person has a job that just isn't a good fit, it becomes very difficult to get out of bed and drag one's self to work each day. More money doesn't change that. My grandmother would have called such a situation, "going against the grain."

I met Bob when he attended the seminar with his sons to help prepare them for the Civil Service test, hoping that they would find a job as secure and well-paying as his was. When the group discussed the personality types, he shared his personal history.

In the early Sixties, Bob struggled to feed his large family. He got a break when he was called to work for the Civil Service as a plumber's apprentice. After completing the apprenticeship program, he was suddenly making twice the hourly income he'd ever made, with vacation and sick benefits that he and his family had only dreamed of. He was able to buy a large home for his wife and eight children, just months after his last child, a daughter, was born.

Bob was also a musician—and this is what he really lived for. He just loved playing for crowds of people and writing new music with his friends, who had performed together since high school.

Finding out that being a plumber was both lonely and boring was a surprise because—after all—a job is just a job. His children, who witnessed his drinking and spouse abuse for years, never associated those character flaws with job dissatisfaction. Bob's generation learned to make the best of having a good job and providing for his family.

The time and energy his job took away from his music left the usually stoic man very angry. He was a people-person—a team worker who longed for immediate approval from others. Plumbers are very important, skilled workers who are appreciated for fixing problems—but they rarely get applause for stopping that toilet from backing up. I pointed out to him that, as lone skilled worker, his personality type made him feel isolated because there was essentially no interaction with people involved. He wasn't suited at all to be working in a self-starting position.

The reaction of his children, when they realized the price their family had all paid for their Dad's job, has stayed with me for years. While it was far too late to change things for Bob, I am glad he brought his sons to the seminar before they took the Civil Service test. They learned their personality type before deciding their own career paths and also gained a new perspective on their father's pain. And talk about a nice graphic illustration for the rest of the class!

There are times when a command-person can't always be in charge, or when a detail-person has to deal with people, or when a people-person has to fill out paperwork, or a support-person has to take over and make a decision. But when self-esteem is weak, it can be a terrifying experience for one personality type to function in the role of another.

Are You Masking Your True Personality?

One serious problem is the masking of a personality type. Some people learn to put forward the outward appearance of a different personality in order to please a disapproving parent or significant other. The result is a severely distorted self-image and weakened self-esteem. If someone is telling you, either directly or indirectly, that who you are is not acceptable, you cannot have a good feeling about yourself.

A command-person may be forced to act as a support-person to keep peace in the family. A people-person child may be deemed unstable by a calm, orderly detail-person parent, when actually the child's unbridled sense of fun is simply getting on the parent's nerves. So, the child tries to act like a detail-person, stifling his real personality and believing he or she is unacceptable and unlovable.

Kevin was a bright, people-person child who was full of so much energy that his support / detail-person mother just couldn't keep up with him. She finally resorted to keeping him up late at night so he would sleep late in the morning so she would have some peace and quiet. Kevin's mother was so desperate for quiet that he grew up feeling guilty about his boisterous sense of humor and bubbly laughter. It finally came to a head when a supervisor asked him and another employee to be quiet one day. Kevin exploded and screamed at the supervisor that he was sick of being told to shut-up all his life. He wasn't fired for this outburst, but he damaged his relationship with the supervisor beyond repair. Eventually, he had to quit his job. Understanding his relationship with his mother and the reasons for her attempts to stifle his natural exuberance would have helped Kevin to react more calmly to the confrontation with his supervisor.

The same thing can happen when an outgoing parent can't understand why his or her introverted child is so quiet and seemingly anti-social. The child may try to put on a happy face and be the clown, but it seldom works. She will become miserable trying to be something she isn't. That can also give the child the idea that no matter how she behaves, she is not going to be successful or acceptable.

Leeann was a quiet detail / support-person. As a child she was shy, had few friends, and rarely spoke to adults in the family at all. In contrast, her command / people-person sister was constantly the center of attention. Leeann began to wonder why she couldn't get the same attention. She tried using some of her sister's dramatic techniques but found that people only laughed and made fun of her. She began to believe that something was wrong with her because she couldn't be as charming and outgoing as her sister. A few more instances of being told she was too quiet and too much of a bookworm contributed to severe relational problems for Leeann at school. It took three years of psychotherapy to help her understand her personality and accept the fact that she had as many valuable strengths as anyone else.

The Test You Cannot Fail

Discovering your true dominant personality type, then accepting its strengths and weaknesses, are key to the development of a healthy self-esteem. The following test is designed to help you determine your type or combination of types.

One way to tell if you are masking your personality is to ask two or three other people who are close to you to fill out the test for you. Compare their analyses of your personality with yours. If they are radically different, you may be masking your true self. You may be telling yourself you are someone else or projecting a false personality to others. Only you can determine which personality is the true one.

On a piece of paper, write headings for "People-Person," "Command-Person," "Detail-Person" and "Support-Person." Go through each column below and write down the words that apply to you most often under the appropriate heading. If you choose a word in one column that also appears in other columns, write it down as many times as it appears. Be spontaneous; try not to think too long about your choices. Then fill in the totals under each column, giving yourself one point for each word. Your highest score is your primary personality; your second highest score, or tie score, indicates your secondary or combination personality.

People-Person	Detail-Person	Command-Person	Support-Person
Convincing	Analytical	Adventurous	Conforming
Cooperative	Cautious	Ambitious	Conscientious
Friendly	Critical	Driving	Meticulous
Generous	Curious	Dominant	Structured
Helpful	Independent	Energetic	Conservative
Intuitive	Inventive	Impulsive	Obedient
Insightful	Intellectual	Optimistic	Orderly
Kind	Introverted	Demanding	Persistent
Popular	Methodical	Self-confident	Practical
Sociable	Precise	Strong-willed	Self-controlled
Tactful	Logical	Enterprising	Indecisive
Understanding	Reserved	Leader	Efficient
Open-minded	Theoretic	Persuasive	Patient
Service-oriented	Experimental	Action-oriented	Thrifty
Imaginative	Perfectionist	Frank	Humble
Impractical	Idealistic	Practical	Modest
Colorful	Complicated	Concrete	Stable
Expressive	Persistent	Innovative	Down-to-earth
Talkative	Listener	Blunt	Empathetic

Remember that people should never be judged solely on their personality type. One type is not better than another, nor is one personality necessarily more valuable to a company than another. Understanding an employee's type is no projection of how that employee will perform on the job. Neither is it an indicator of loyalty, dedication or moral standards.

Using personality tests to screen or eliminate employees—rather than to discover the best use of their abilities—is improper. It is simply a tool to facilitate understanding of how a person approaches situations, problems and decisions. Use the personality types to help you understand why people do what they do, not to judge them for what they do.

All personality types have strengths and weaknesses. Some people have more of the strengths, and some have more of the weaknesses than others with the same personality type. But all pieces fit into the puzzle and complete the big picture.

Applying these principles specifically to your job will be discussed in depth in the following chapters *How to Love the Co-worker You Hate* and *How to Love the Boss You Hate.*

CHAPTER FOUR
HOW TO LOVE THE BOSS YOU HATE

Perhaps there is no love lost when it comes to the relationship with your manager. You hate him or her, and you're pretty sure they don't care for you either. You are not alone in your feelings.

A few years ago, General Electric did some studies on why their workers were satisfied or not with their jobs. They discovered a connection between job satisfaction and worker / boss communication. Five key topics were identified as central to that communication: discussion of work-related problems, informal feedback on performance, informal feedback on salary and / or career discussions and performance appraisals.

Ninety percent of the employees who believed the five areas were well covered by their bosses expressed overall job satisfaction. GE's conclusion was employees who were least satisfied were those who were not well-managed. That probably doesn't surprise you—especially if you are working with a boss right now who is less than communicative.

The following quiz is designed to bring your relationship with your boss into focus, particularly in the crucial area of communication. On a sheet of paper, number 1-15. For each question, write down the number that best describes your reaction to the question: 4-excellent; 3-good; 2-satisfactory; 1-needs improvement; 0-unsatisfactory. When you are through, add up all the numbers to come up with the score for your boss.

1. Your boss makes you feel valuable to her or him and to your organization.

2. Your boss clearly communicates the performance required for you

to be successful in your job.

3. Your boss clearly communicates what he wants you to do on a particular project.

4. Your boss listens to your ideas and implements them when appropriate.

5. Your boss gives you credit for your ideas when they are implemented and prove to be successful.

6. Your boss sets reasonable deadlines.

7. Your boss makes changes in priorities only when it is necessary.

8. Your boss makes fair decisions about performance appraisals, promotions, salary increases and bonuses.

9. Your boss avoids negative confrontations with you.

10. Your boss considers your viewpoint when making decisions that affect you.

11. Your boss listens to you.

12. Your boss learns from his or her own mistakes.

13. Your boss gives you honest, constructive feedback about your work—even when it's not positive.

14. Your boss avoids playing power games when possible.

15. Your boss does his job in such a way that you can live with his flaws.

Score	Conclusion
60-48	You like working with your boss. You are obviously reading this chapter because it is part of the book—not because you are having difficulties. Count your blessings and file it in your "me" file for a reference when you become a supervisor.
47-25	Not bad at all. By taking an active role, you stand a chance of creating a more satisfying relationship with your boss. This chapter can help you understand your boss better and seek ways to rectify any existing or future problems.
24-11	It doesn't hurt to try taking some positive steps, but more than likely you need to hang on until you can pursue another opportunity. Learning about your boss's temperament in this chapter should provide you with some coping mechanisms.

10-0	Uh-oh. This could be the main reason why you hate your job. Think about leaving your present position (if you haven't already). Most likely you're in a situation where the best solution may be to move on as soon as you can

Techniques of Good Management

Before you take positive steps toward improving your relationship with your boss, it is important to understand what a good boss really is—what, in fact, constitutes good management. Here are six points that have been recognized as the essence of good management. Keep these techniques in mind while you try to develop a stronger working relationship with your boss.

1. An Effective Boss Builds an Atmosphere of Open Communication

The GE survey mentioned earlier states that open communication is a major factor in employee satisfaction. You must be able to approach and talk openly with your boss. Does your boss say she has an open door policy? Is she accessible, or do you find her reluctant to deal with any problems that you mention? Is she sending a double message—is what she saying really, "My door is always open, but don't bother me if you don't have to"? That is quite common.

An effective manager invites suggestions and even constructive criticism. Instead of waiting for you to initiate communication, they may solicit feedback and discuss current problems and possible solutions. He or she may have implemented some type of formal or informal survey process to understand how employees are doing and feeling about their current jobs.

An exceptional manager cares about the employee and realizes that worker feedback is critical for the productivity of the organization. Not every manager is willing to take that time, however. Every working person should feel that management is willing to listen. In order to achieve employee satisfaction, goals and expectations must be clarified; constructive guidance and direction provided when appropriate.

2. Trust Is Critical to a Good Working Relationship

Is your boss honest and fair? Does he level with you, even when it might reflect negatively on him or the organization? Does he follow through on his promises? Has he taken the time to evaluate his own strengths and weaknesses as well as yours?

Recall from the first chapter the example of Carole who was working for a trucking company. New regulations were causing difficulties. Carole's supervisors had stopped inviting her to critical meetings. Obviously, they were uncertain about their situation and didn't want Carole to know how bad things were. By not taking her into their confidence, they missed a chance to utilize Carole's special expertise, which may have provided a solution to their dilemma. As a result of this tension, Carole and her assistant Leah became more fearful of their work environment, which in turn affected their personal relationship. All in all, it was a real lose-lose situation for everyone. Had the supervisors trusted their employees, things would have evolved much differently.

The best bosses deal with their employees in the way in which they would like to be dealt. Supervisors convey genuine respect by being straightforward in their communications and following through on promises. An employee's feeling about their work, no matter how insignificant, is important to Management. They deal fairly with each employee, not allowing favoritism or personality differences to affect their judgment. When a worker trusts their boss, they are motivated to greater productivity, achievement and loyalty.

3. A Supportive Environment Motivates the Employees

A boss who says, "We are a team; we work together," creates a sense of security for the employee. Workers are openly appreciated when appropriate. They are constructively corrected—privately—when necessary. Problem-solving is a mutual effort. A boss should be willing to use his or her influence and even go to bat for the employee with higher-ups when appropriate. Employees who have that kind of support rarely get into trouble, because they have the direction, information and tools they need in order to do their job. They also have self-confidence and do a good job, knowing the boss's support is there like a safety net if they make an honest mistake. A supportive boss has compassion and empathy for his employees.

4. A Supportive Boss Has a Genuine Interest in Workers as Individuals

A supportive boss takes the time to get to know each employee's personality, needs, goals and learns something about the employee's personal life.

Such bosses get the optimal performance from each person because they are able to bring out each employee's unique abilities. They recognize that some people need closer supervision than others do. They design tasks and working conditions around the individual needs of the employee. These sorts of supervisors, who are able to make their people feel important and personally significant, also generate the most productivity and loyalty.

Now we come back to Kenny's story. Kenny is not only the best kind of employee—answering the call of duty to constantly be on the go, visiting each customer to make sure they stay with the company—but he could also be the most dangerous employee. He has a family he rarely sees and a wife with a young son she is caring for all alone, with no family or friends nearby. His company is competitive and safe from other businesses because of Kenny's tenacity with customer service. Yet not one of his bosses seems to realize that. If the pressure begins to get to Kenny and he allows just one client to feel the same sense of abandonment as he does, business could begin to slide, placing everyone's job in jeopardy. Why does no one seem to care enough to be more supportive to Kenny? Has anyone asked how this schedule affects his family life? Kenny's job has expanded so much that he cannot possibly keep up, yet his supervisors seem totally unaware of it.

It is only a matter of time until headhunters of the competition find out that there is just one man standing in the way of their own prosperity. Other companies would no doubt offer Kenny the proverbial moon, including a small staff of workers he could train and supervise to do the job he is doing right now. Kenny feels that he has excellent benefits, but those benefits were originally offered to a single man, when Kenny was much younger and had totally different needs. Since he spends so much time traveling, his family could live almost anywhere on his travel route, so his wife could live in a city where she has more support and familiarity.

There are other benefit options besides actual moving expenses that could help this family that has moved so often. A creative personnel officer or business owner should design benefit packages that best support company employees. Over time, Kenny will probably chose his family, if it comes down to that, over a company that refuses to see him as a person. Kenny's bosses have so much to lose by ignoring the personal needs of this valuable employee. His supervisor should become an advocate to help Kenny—if only to save his own job. A personnel problem such as this is easily prevented by following techniques of good management

5. A Good Boss Helps Each Employee Reach Their Potential

A manager should do whatever is possible to develop each employee to his or her fullest potential. Goal setting and career planning are integral in this process. A good boss increases employee's responsibilities and encourages their independence. Creativity is stimulated as opposed to demanding adherence to rules and prescribed patterns. The boss can take a vacation and not worry about the department coming to a standstill.

Mark, from the first chapter, is living in paradise and after about seven years will soon reach his long-term goal of receiving his MBA. His boss has been rather lavish with resort resources to show Mark appreciation for his many years of work as a bartender. But he assumes that Mark will welcome the job in accounting and stay on with the company. In all his years of employment, Mark's boss has no idea what goals were initially set and what it might take to change those goals in favor of working at the resort. If asked, his boss would say that Mark is a great bartender who went to college and is ready to be promoted into a different department at the resort. The supervisor might add that Mark has a family in the Midwest—but that's about all he knows. The truth is the boss doesn't even know that Mark is looking at offers in downtown Honolulu. He actually does not really know Mark at all.

This supervisor might see a completely different career for Mark—if he knew what was happening. Mark's years of experience as a rank-and-file union worker, plus his graduate degree in business, would make him a valuable negotiator, representing the resort in union talks and mediations. How can a manager envision a career path for a subordinate without taking the time to know him or her?

6. A Good Boss Gives Feedback

Giving and receiving feedback is one of the most important aspects of an employee / boss relationship. Whether it comes from written evaluations, informal or formal discussions, or occasional memos, feedback should be given on a regular basis. How can you know how you're doing unless your boss tells you? A good supervisor makes sure his people get adequate timely feedback on what they are doing—right or wrong.

Research shows that positive rewards and appreciation motivate employees. They are far more effective than demoralizing threats and punishment. That is why bosses who recognize their employees' accomplishments are usually far more effective than those who have a reputation for being tough on their employees are. However, when unpleasant feedback must be given, it should focus on the inappropriate behavior, not the person as an individual. Just because the employee makes a mistake, does not mean the employee *is* a mistake.

Manage Your Boss for a Change

Many of the major complaints people have about their jobs could be solved at the worker / boss level. A boss who incorporates these six points into his or her management style can have a positive impact on how an employee feels about his job.

How do you get your boss to incorporate these ideas? By managing your boss. Take an active role in that relationship. Don't wait for your boss to change his response to you; change your response to your boss. Instead of a passive non-response, determine how you will approach your boss based on your understanding of his management style. You can't control your boss, but you can control your own attitudes, emotions, and work style. Think of yourself as the manager—because you are, in this case!

Janet was a bookkeeper in the accounting department of a large company. She was very unhappy with her job and was experiencing stress-related illnesses. The primary source of her unhappiness was her boss, Dave.

Dave was a people-person who would never say no, so he constantly lied about the status of his work. The result was that Janet often got caught in his lies. For more than a year, she tried to hide her negative feelings about her job, assuming that the only thing she could do was wait.

Before she resigned, she blew up and confronted Dave about his lying. In response he almost fired her. She carried her unresolved frustration with her until she moved on to another job.

How do you avoid ticking away like a time bomb in anger and frustration at your boss? It helps if your boss is open to working on the relationship— something Dave wasn't willing to do with Janet. But if your supervisor seems to be unwilling, remember that your attitude is what is important. A negative, accusatory, or disgruntled attitude will only make things worse. It's also best not to try to approach your boss when you are angry. That only adds to the bad feelings rather than alleviating them.

Instead of smoldering in dissatisfaction, ask your boss when the two of you can talk without interruption. You might say, "I would like to talk to you about how I can do my job better. I think this could benefit both of us. Do you have some time this week when we could talk? I would really be interested in your input." That way, it doesn't sound like you want to have a complaint session.

When you go in to talk with your boss, know specifically what you want to talk about. Clarify the issues in your mind first, then write them down. If you need to point out a problem area, especially if it concerns something the boss is or is not doing right, offer a suggestion as to how you could help solve it.

"I know you've been very busy lately and haven't had time to do my performance appraisal. It would really help me do a better job if I could get your input through an evaluation. Maybe I could stay late and take one or two tasks off your hands to free up some time for you."

Remember, too, empathy and understanding is a two-way street. Put yourself in you boss's shoes. Is you boss under a lot of stress? I can't imagine very many bosses who aren't in these economically troubled times. Increasing numbers of managers are suffering from burnout due to the intense pressure they are getting from those above them. Unfortunately, since more and more companies are bottom-line oriented, they don't appreciate the long-term benefits of having caring, people-oriented managers. Your boss may sincerely want to make things better but feels frustrated in his efforts by top management.

Here is where you can manage your boss. Offer support and you will likely get support in return. Believe it or not, he or she is human, too! Ask what you can do to help make his job easier. Be willing to take on some tasks that you may not like. Later, you may get a chance to do something you really want to do.

You don't have to be a doormat and let her dump all her problems on you. And it certainly would not do to let her suspect that you have too much free time in your own job. But you can try making an exchange. Maybe her desk is piled high with things she doesn't have time to file. That is just one more stress element that makes her feel she doesn't have time to help you. Offer to clear her desk so she will have time to train you in an area you want to learn.

If you can show your boss that you are willing to give as much effort as possible, you just might earn his respect, even in a difficult relationship. After all, the feedback you give your boss may be just the information he needed to do his job better. Don't be afraid to speak up when your motives are sincerely oriented toward improving your job.

Once the communication ball is rolling, don't let it lose momentum. When you and your boss have set some goals, check regularly to see how things are progressing. You might want to take a few minutes after work once a week to check in. Your boss will know that you meant business and that your efforts were not just a momentary whim.

Here are some other tips to remember when communicating with your boss:

- Develop a specific list of wants that the boss can reasonably implement.

- Turn the tables: give your boss sincere, appropriate appreciation. Make sure it is sincere. People know when it is not real.

- Don't be demanding. If you appear to be unwilling to negotiate about your wants, your appeal will fall on deaf ears.

- Be open and honest. You may walk out of a meeting with your boss without getting all your wants, but you will still have your most valuable asset; your integrity.

On some occasions you may try everything with your boss without getting anywhere. What do you do next? You may want to go to your boss's boss, but be very careful about going over his head. It could cause resentment and damage your relationship even further. However, it may be the only way around an "immovable object." Don't let yourself be trapped by a boss who is unwilling to give you an honest chance to improve your situation.

Understand Your Boss's Temperament

As your forge a new relationship with your boss, it is important to know his or her personality style or temperament to accelerate the communication process. The following is a brief discussion of the four personalities as they relate to a leadership style.

If your boss is a command-person, the best way to communicate with him is to be brief, clear and to the point. Present your ideas as concrete goals, back up your reasoning with facts but not a lot of data, and cite examples of success.

Command-persons are least receptive to anything that appears to be unproductive or a waste of time, including attempts at relationship-building that are not related to a specific work objective. They are not interested in small talk. Be as organized and logical as possible in your approach. More than any other temperament, command-persons appreciate loyalty to their policies and to the company.

Jim, a command-person, is the owner of a software company. His bottom-line, results-oriented style of management could be seen as aggressive and insensitive to his employees. But the wise employees have learned to respond appropriately to Jim. For instance, when work on a major project hits an obstacle, Jim's employees know that he sees it as a challenge. Thus, they react by presenting solutions to the problem clearly, briefly, and always with the understanding that failure isn't even in Jim's vocabulary—therefore, it isn't in his employee's vocabulary, either. The project will succeed, and Jim (and it follows, his employees) will be happy. This approach applies to working out the obstacles in the employees' relationships with Jim: by mirroring his no-nonsense style, employees see Jim respond in turn with more encouragement and less overly-demanding behavior.

A sort of saving grace Jim has given his employees who came to understand him is that, no matter what goes wrong, he will never give up and is willing to work with everyone to fix it. His employees have a strong sense of loyalty to a boss that won't allow things to go wrong for very long. He has given them confidence and job security without ever promising a thing. He has modeled it for them.

If your boss is a people-person, be prepared to listen—and listen and listen! People-persons are interested in small talk, especially when they are doing it. Approach this boss in a friendly way, and present your ideas as creatively as possible. Don't deal heavily in facts, figures or risks. After you have shared your idea, you may find your boss embellishing it with his own. Don't try to cling rigidly to your original idea. Be flexible, and you will be more likely to gain acceptance.

Compliment the people-person on his insight and inventiveness, and you will find him responsive to your needs. You may also have to drop a few gentle reminders now and then, because when he gets interested in another project, yours may slip his mind. This temperament is the one that will most sincerely want to see you happy, as he loves pleasing people. Sometimes he forgets to follow through, however, because he is off on another idea. Remember not to take that as a personal slight and you should get along famously.

The benefit for employees of a people-person is that their door is almost always open and they usually will listen to new ideas and share your excitement, if at all possible. So, take heart, when he or she starts on another story and keep one eye on a new project that could propel you into a new career path.

If your boss is a detail-person, he is just the opposite of a people-person. This boss expects accuracy, objectivity and practical guarantees against risk. If you want him to try something new, you should provide a detailed analysis as to why it should be done and how it will work. The detail-person tends to communicate in a direct, businesslike manner and does not often appreciate a casual attitude or inappropriate humor. He may, in fact, appear curt and cold but is simply more comfortable with facts and figures than polished salesmanship.

Leslie is a detail-person designer for an architectural firm. She supervises one employee who, at times, finds Leslie's desire for accuracy irritating and even bordering on compulsive. However, after assessing Leslie's detail-oriented temperament, the employee has been able to develop a satisfying relationship by providing thorough analyses and updates for Leslie on each project they share. The employee also learned that Leslie responds best to direct communication and ongoing, thorough discussion regarding the employee's concerns; especially when the discussion involves practical solutions that are well-thought-out and presented without extreme emotional displays.

The detail-person boss is the most straightforward one to manage. Do your homework and leave your excitement about the project at home, and you should be fine.

If your boss is a support-person, he, like the detail-person, may not be comfortable in a leadership position. When trying to initiate communication, be as non-threatening as possible. Be patient and take the time to show personal interest. Develop the relationship. Don't be abrupt or too businesslike. Support-people are friendly, but they are not usually outgoing.

It is best to avoid areas of strong disagreement. Support-people do not like conflict. When suggesting new ideas, emphasize your assistance or that of other people. She will like other people's ideas. Also, when she has to initiate a change or a project, she needs to know that others will cooperate with her. It is easy to get along with a support-person when there is no conflict, but she is likely to clam up if you appear disagreeable. She likes to keep things peaceful and harmonious, so she will usually be encouraging. Remember that the support-person does not push, so you may not always get fast results.

Most people are a combination of two of these temperaments. Your boss will probably fall into two styles. You can't always identify the secondary temperament, but the primary one should be fairly obvious. The important thing to remember is that, unless your boss is the same temperament as you (which can cause its own problems), you each have a different way of approaching your job, your relationship and your life. That does not make either of you inherently right or wrong, just different.

If you are a detail- or support-person, a command- or people-person may intimidate you. A command-person may seem rigid, impersonal, and autocratic to a gentle support-person who only wants to please others and avoid decisions. A people-person may seem flashy and impractical to a careful, quiet detail-person who prefers to be factual and precise. On the other hand, the support-person probably seems wishy-washy and irritatingly slow to the dynamic, hard-driving command-person. And the detail-person can seem a dogmatic bore to the enthusiastic, fun-loving people-person.

Think about your reactions. Are you really having problems with your boss? Is he or she trying to ruin your life—or is he just being the natural-born leader his temperament is designed to be? When you understand your own and your boss's temperaments and how they interact, you are on the road to better communication already.

Each temperament has a function and particular role to play. In managing your boss, remember that if you're a detail- or support-person feeling intimidated by a command-person or people-person boss, then he needs you! Who would carry out the commands of the command-person if there were no support-persons? Conversely, who would delegate and discuss projects if there were no command- or people-persons?

Understanding and appreciating differences is vital to managing your boss. You may feel that it is too much responsibility and work to figure out your boss—that your boss should make more of an effort to understand you. In an ideal world, your goal is to make your relationship with your boss as solid and open as it can be by doing your part.

CHAPTER FIVE

HOW TO LOVE THE CO-WORKER YOU HATE

Karen, a junior account executive at a public relations firm, dreads the company's weekly staff meetings. The reason is Rex, one of her co-workers. Rex is also an account executive, but as far as Karen is concerned, that is where any similarities between she and Rex end. She finds Rex obnoxious, opinionated and rude. Her list of complaints against him is fairly lengthy. In fact, Karen so strongly dislikes Rex that she avoids contact with him in every way possible, which is why the weekly staff meetings are so uncomfortable.

"We are not," Karen says, with a wan smile, *"simpatico."* Despite her ironic tone, there is an edge of despair in her voice—her intense dislike of Rex definitely causes her stress on the job, and she wishes she could do something about it.

Working in the same Public Relations agency, Chip is a staff paste-up artist who has his own co-worker struggles with Benjamin, a writer. Tight deadlines and high profile projects—the bread and butter for PR firms—are normal at the agency. Chip constantly runs into problems with Benjamin's inability to get the work done on time. Try as he might, Chip cannot get Benjamin to cooperate with him, which in turn, hinders Chip's performance. Chip deeply resents Benjamin and is at the point of going to the writer's superior to complain.

Let's say that, like Karen and Chip, you are contending with a difficult work situation. It is not your boss—you like him or her. It is not your workload—you are handling that well. You are even learning to love whatever other aspects of the job you hated when you started. But when it comes to that particular person you work with, you may be asking yourself, "Can I ever really love the co-worker I hate?" The answer may seem to be no, yet it can be a resounding *yes.* You can love the colleague you hate, but it will probably take some effort.

It will take work because in difficult circumstances it is never easy to change; particularly when the person who must decide to make the change is you.

The work environment can be loosely compared to a family. As co-workers, you are together a substantial part of your waking hours. You depend on one another to meet mutual goals. You are a group of people with distinct personalities and needs. As with any family, there are conflicts. But the blood ties and years of togetherness that bond a family together through difficulties probably do not exist in your work situation. So other factors must come into play in order to create a harmonious, productive environment.

With that in mind, let's get more specific about your work environment. Think about your work team now, instead of a family. When you think "team," you picture what dictionaries define as *a group of people, working together, toward a common goal, according to a structured plan.*

The future of America's companies will require that workers no longer be islands unto themselves, but functioning units pulling together for greater productivity and a sweeter bottom line. Even if you are not technically part of a group of people working on a specific project together, you may be looking for the togetherness that comes from sharing a common interest—success on the job. When you make it your goal to work successfully as a team member, you are developing a foundation for success in even the most unstable co-worker relationship. It takes time though, and a willingness to apply new thinking to an old problem. That new thinking begins with a list of things you can do to develop a team relationship with the co-worker you are struggling to love.

Communicate

Or rather: communicate, communicate, communicate! That is how important communicating is in helping to turn around the negative relationship you have with your co-worker. In fact, it is the umbrella for everything that happens as you seek to establish a more positive relationship with your colleague. What you do and say, how you look and sound, must be consistent and clear. Even if you only talk about work and never get into conversations of a personal nature, you can establish and maintain excellent communication.

Karen disliked Rex for so long and with such intensity that she did little to hide her feelings around him. She let others know how she felt but never directed any comments to Rex. Because there was no way for Rex to address Karen's feelings about him, he goaded her. He became more obnoxious, hoping he could force a confrontation with Karen and that she would address her feelings about him, directly. Until then, he knew of no other way to act around her, other than trying to get her attention. Rex admitted to himself that he actually liked Karen. In the beginning, he acted out just to get her to notice him. From the start, Karen's body language and curt answers to his questions let him know exactly how she felt. That left him hurt and embarrassed. When others repeated her comments to him, he didn't know how to react. The problem between the two of them went from bad to worse. Since neither of them addressed it with each other, it looked liked it would stay that way until one or the other of them quit their job.

After talking to Karen and getting her permission to speak frankly with Rex, I got them to sit down with me. My job was just to mediate and I encouraged them to pretend I wasn't there. Karen was able to tell Rex how she felt. She had noticed his admiration of her when he first came to work, but she didn't know what to make of this kind of attention in the workplace. She resented being in that situation. Since Rex never acted out in a way that could be labeled sexual harassment, Karen felt guilty when she knew she was being so mean to him.

Rex apologized and admitted that he acted immaturely. His honesty allowed Karen to feel some empathy for him. They never did become friends, but they were able to move on and work well together. Their co-workers noticed the difference with the tension gone. All it took to end this office upheaval was honest, direct communication.

If you have a co-worker who seems to misinterpret constantly what you are telling him or her about what you need, examine your conversations. Are you being clear? Are you being direct? Are you listening to their questions and are they answering yours? Sometimes it is a simple matter of slowing down your way of speaking to present your needs. Do you make others work to understand you? Keep your communication simple and to the point. Then his work should improve, which should improve your attitude toward him.

Listen

This is the other side of the communication coin. Let your colleague teach you something about him. Of course, listening involves more than just letting your co-worker's comments go in one ear, only to drift out of the other once you leave his presence. Listening means you retain the information, consider it useful and learn about your co-worker from what he or she tells you.

When you listen to your colleague do you *appear* to be paying attention? What does your body language say about your listening skills? Do you keep eye contact, stop what you are doing and give her your full attention? This is a problem for supervisors when they are trying to help or train a worker. If the worker is shy or intimidated and looks at the ground while the supervisor is speaking to them, the boss may repeat the training or never be sure that the worker understood. This is frustrating for both and it can escalate into a genuine personnel problem. Make sure your co-worker knows you are listening by being animated, using eye-contact and, just to be sure, ask a question or repeat what you have been told by way of feedback so they know you have heard them.

When your co-worker sees that you are truly involved in what he is saying, he will respond to you in kind by listening to you. You will discover the give-and-take of true communication, which can only serve to help build a healthy, working relationship.

Try a Little Respect

You should ask yourself, "Would my co-worker say he gets no respect from me?" This is not a question of whether he *deserves* your respect. You should treat that person as a human being, deserving of your respect—which is your consideration and regard for him as a person. This can go a long way toward improving your attitude about your co-worker.

In the case of Karen and Rex, Karen's body language and facial expressions were all anyone in the staff meetings needed to know that she detested him. In front of all of their co-workers and supervisor, she scowled and folded her arms, conveying her feelings every time Rex began to express an idea. She never said a word. The tension made everyone uncomfortable. Rex, feeling very embarrassed, would start to ramble and make matters worse. The disrespect Karen showed to her co-worker disrupted every staff meeting, and yet she felt it was Rex, alone, who made the meetings a nightmare.

Examine Your Contribution to Negative Relationships

Examine your own reaction to your co-workers. Are you creating conflict that doesn't exist except in your own mind? Are you reacting defensively to a co-worker's unthinking comment and letting it fester? The key to making a difference in your relationship with your co-workers is simply to talk with them and let them explain their position. Again, communicate and take care to listen openly, giving the person your full attention. Clear your mind of preconceived notions.

Recognize Your Differences

How do you cope with a difficult co-worker? Do you think she is lazy and uncooperative? Does a particular colleague always manage to take credit for your work? Or does she seem to be the boss's pet, always getting the plum assignments and privileges, while you languish in your cubicle with the most boring work?

Consider this: some of what you perceive about difficult people in your job could be your own inability to recognize that your co-worker is simply different than you. Remember the personality types. Though each type plays its own role on a job, some specific traits in each will annoy some of the others.

For instance, people-persons and detail-persons are opposites, and they sometimes find it difficult to understand each other. That is the case with Karen and her co-worker, Rex. Karen is primarily a detail-person, quietly servicing her clients. She is effective on her job despite a less commanding presence than many others in her position. Rex, on the other hand, is a combination people-person / command-person. His hard-driving, "center-of-attention" personality seems obnoxious to Karen and, if she were to admit it, a little intimidating. Karen must decide to accept—and try to understand—Rex's strengths as well as his weaknesses. By focusing on his strengths, she can understand why he fits into his job and reach a level of comfort in her own.

You should not expect to become the best of friends with a co-worker whom you find difficult. Karen and Rex may never go out to lunch as buddies, but if she attempts to understand his personality better, she will be able to learn from him. She can communicate effectively with him in and outside of staff meetings, and enjoy her job that much more.

As you examine the personality type of your difficult co-worker, ask yourself if that person might even be in the wrong position for his or her personality. If that is the case, there is nothing you can do about it unless you become the person's supervisor. Then you could save the day for both of you by gently guiding the person into another, more type-appropriate, career path.

Give Up the Need for Control

Whether you're the quiet detail-person or the action-oriented command-person, most people who are struggling with a difficult co-worker want to do something to "fix" that person—to change him or her into what you think they should be. To put it bluntly, forget it! The only person who can change in a co-worker crisis is *you*. You cannot expect to control your colleague's behavior without causing further conflict and tension for both of you.

Chip, the paste-up artist at the PR firm, had to come to that conclusion. He wanted desperately to turn Benjamin, the writer, into an organized, conscientious person who would help his own job go smoother. But Chip realized that the Pygmalion approach wouldn't work on Benjamin. How can he gain some control over what he felt was an out-of-control situation?

First, he can have a confrontation with Benjamin that is as direct and tactful as possible. Chip has never asked Benjamin why he gets behind in his work or told him how his tardiness creates problems for him. Instead, Chip has only hinted to Benjamin that there were some problems with deadlines. A more productive approach is to ask questions such as, "How will you catch up so that we will meet the deadline?" "What can I do so that there aren't further problems?" Approaching the situation with the team concept in mind—that is, offering a "we" solution to the problem as opposed to a "you" solution—might help Chip resolve the conflict.

Should Benjamin prove to be completely uncooperative, Chip may then chose to seek conflict resolution through mediators, such as their supervisors. Although Chip's initial instinct is to paint Benjamin in the worst possible light, he would find that by leaving the discipline in the hands of Benjamin's superior, he will avoid further tension.

Once you decide to change yourself and let go of your attempts to control your co-worker, be casual in your approach to relationship building, as any sudden change in your behavior may breed suspicion. Your co-worker may begin to wonder, "Now what is she after?" You don't want that response. In an already difficult relationship, the other person may be naturally suspicious of you anyway. Take it slowly and do not make demands. Just let the person know that you really want to work out the relationship to benefit both of you.

Some Other Points to Consider

Praise has power. Praising a co-worker has the power to change both of you. Unless you are totally unable to find something to congratulate or praise a difficult co-worker for, telling her that she is doing a good job can be a true relationship builder. Not only will your co-worker respond positively, but you will be reminded about the good things she is capable of, which can create a warming trend in a chilly relationship.

Where's your sense of humor? Laughter is another power source in boosting a relationship with a difficult co-worker. Do you have a shared experience that is funny? Laugh about it together. Do you have a good, clean joke that the other person might enjoy? Open up and tell it. Even when your co-worker says something that traditionally annoys you, decide to smile about it and keep on going. (That is not hypocrisy, by the way; it is self-preservation.)

Empathize. It isn't easy—it even hurts a little sometimes—but try to step into that difficult co-worker's shoes. Does he have a boss that irritates him and therefore makes him irritating for you to work with? Is he obviously struggling with personal problems that are affecting his behavior on the job? Empathy can cover a multitude of sins, giving you a deeper awareness of conflicts that could be causing your co-worker to be the difficult person he is being.

While working as a consultant for their company, I was asked to mediate the conflicts affecting Chip and Benjamin's work. Since their team consistently failed to meet deadlines, the supervisors asked me to interview both of them. The supervisors told me that Benjamin's wife had suffered a mental breakdown. Since this problem was personal, neither supervisor was willing to tell Chip about the burden of stress that Benjamin was working under. He was afraid each time he left the house in the morning, and scrambled to find relatives and friends to sit with his wife. When Benjamin finally did make it to work, he was still working under considerable personal stress. Unfortunately, he was oblivious to the feelings of others and did his job as best he could.

This consultation was a good one on many levels because I asked the supervisors if the company was really doing all it could to ease the burden for Benjamin. One supervisor mentioned an Employee Assistance Program that had been included in the corporate medical plan, but that nobody had ever used it because they weren't quite sure of its function. While they looked into that, I sat down with Benjamin and discretely told him that others in his work team were feeling frustrated about actions by one person that reflected on everyone.

Benjamin said that his biggest fear was that if he could not work, he would not be able to provide medical care for his wife. He felt isolated at his job but did not want to burden others with his personal struggles. He could not see how a regular mediation could protect was his wife's privacy, fearing that comments would be made behind his back about her mental illness. After all, while we may expect empathy for the disabilities of others, we still can't trust that all people are that tolerant.

Benjamin and I finally came to an agreement about what I could say. I told Chip that Benjamin was working under a heavy personal burden that he wanted kept quiet. I let Chip know that the supervisors were apprized of the situation and should be able to provide some help through company benefits. My conclusion to Chip was that, if he could just hang on a bit, help was on the way; his boss was aware that the deadline problems were *not* his fault. Lastly, I advised him that common courtesy and empathy in the voices of his co-workers would be helpful to Benjamin. Chip was more than willing to take my advice and ask Benjamin, "How can I help us meet this deadline?" When I checked back with the supervisors a month later, the team was meeting deadlines and working on building better working relationships.

Forgive. One of the main themes in this book is to do unto others as you would have them do unto you. Remembering that concept as you deal with a difficult co-worker is vital. When you make a mistake, you want forgiveness. Perhaps you were damaged emotionally or professionally. What a freeing feeling you get when you forgive that co-worker any wrongs he or she has done to you. Holding a grudge is never productive and only serves to build tension.

When I sat down with Chip and gave him only basic information about what Benjamin was going through, his body language changed completely. He sat back in his chair and his facial expression displayed that of a person with compassion. I could see that, for Chip, the problem was over. And for Benjamin the problem can, at least, be better at work as he now feels subtle support from his teammates.

Forgive and try to let go. You may be pleasantly surprised by the feeling of peace that often follows.

Know When to Cut Your Losses. You hope that you won't have to give up on improving a difficult relationship with a co-worker, but sometimes there is just no resolving the conflict. Short of quitting your job, the solutions are somewhat limited. However, you can request a transfer out of the department. You can approach the person's supervisor about the problem and perhaps gain some insight into the person that you did not have. Then you have to leave it in the supervisor's hands. You can hope that the person will be removed from your immediate vicinity. Or you can simply grin and bear it, keeping in mind that you must respect that person's difference from you. In time, you can train yourself not to respond at all to his or her difficult behavior.

On a Positive Note

The Benefits of Becoming a Team. Although it was noted earlier that you will not always—and may not even want to—become friends with the co-worker you hate, there is a good chance that you can turn a rocky relationship into a golden one. As you seek to build that team, you can discover some important benefits from your improved relationship.

Support. Co-workers—or your work teammates—offer the sweetest reward on any job. If you have established your own strengths and weaknesses and respect those of your teammates, not one of you can fail. You can all celebrate those moments of victory:

- When you hit the deadline.

- Bring in the new client.

- Your department reaches the end of the year under your expense budget

- You have stronger than projected sales.

- Your section has the fewest "days-lost injuries."

- Your machinery has the lowest number of "status down days."

- Your team creates its own warm and wonderful feeling of accomplishment.

The best kind of support you can offer your colleagues is the surety that you can hold up your end of the project. That's all you really have to do, and that in turn creates trust. The team that has trust among its members will be unbeatable, and competing companies know this. That's why successful employers plan for activities that foster team-building. After all, the team victory goes to the team manager and coaches, as well.

Acceptance. Once that bridge of hostility has been crossed, acceptance is on the other side. You accept your co-workers for who they are, not what you want them to be, or even what they could be. They accept you the same way. Acceptance frees one up from the stress of hostility. It promotes a healthier workplace for everyone.

Openness. Being open means being vulnerable, but it also means you can circumvent hidden agendas, suspicious behavior and fear of reprisal when you discuss your concerns. No one can be open without trust. When a co-worker becomes a team member, and one of the ground rules for which all have agreed is openness, then all can expect the nurturing rewards of an honest and cohesive relationship. There is also the extra benefit of always knowing that your co-workers are not angry with you or talking about you behind your back, because everyone feels free to tell you how you may have hurt their feelings before it grows into anger.

Professional Satisfaction. Finally, the decks have been cleared. Now you can get on with the business of doing the best job you can. If you have been effective in improving your relationship with your co-worker, you now have an ally. Your job should be easier when you are not carrying around the burdens of tension, anger, worry, resentment and so on. Your work will seem richer and more rewarding when you have resolved the conflict with your co-worker in a professional, carefully thought-out manner.

CHAPTER SIX

HOW TO LOVE THE COMPANY YOU HATE

Companies, businesses and organizations come in all sizes and shapes. From massive corporations with international offices to medium-sized companies with a few hundred employees to small businesses with less that twenty-five people, the organizational structure, culture and philosophy is as important to success as the quality of products and services.

Is your company big and tightly organized? Do you have to get permission from your supervisor's supervisor to purchase a few paper clips? Or is your company small and chaotic, with everyone doing his own thing and hoping it all falls into place? Perhaps you think there is just the right amount of structure, providing adequate supervision and guidance, yet with enough freedom to be innovative?

Is the culture of your organization one of strict attention to business, with formal rules and dress codes? Does it promote some flexibility in how you dress, carry out your duties and communicate with your supervisors and co-workers? Or is it so lax that it borders on being unprofessional?

What about your company's philosophy? Ethics? Values? Does it put customers first? Does it value and support the employees? Is it concerned about being environmentally responsible? Does it believe in contributing to the needs of the community? Or is it strictly a profit-making venture? Are its ethics questionable in its pursuit of profits?

All of these things must be considered when you are evaluating your feelings about your job. How does your work style fit with your organizational structure? How does your personality fit with the corporate culture? Do the company's ethics reflect your own values, or do they conflict with yours? Let's examine each of these aspects of the workplace and look at how they affect your job satisfaction.

Structure: Too Big, Too Small or Just Right?

Though size was once considered a sign of prosperity and stability for a company, today it is becoming a liability. Downsizing and to a "lean and mean" model is the prevalent trend in business now. Many giant corporations have slashed thousands of jobs in an effort to be more competitive. Layers of middle management have been eliminated to bring decision-making closer to the workers.

What does all that mean for employees? The people who do the work and deal with customers every day will have more involvement in how the company operates. Ultimately, workers will have to take more responsibility for the company's success.

That can have positive results, allowing employees to develop their abilities more fully, stretch their skills and enjoy the rewards of personal and professional growth. But it can also be scary. If you work for a big company and believe that it is your "security blanket," you may someday find that your blanket has been thrown out. Now is a good time to look at the big picture in your company.

Begin preparing yourself to be more actively involved in the operations and decision-making. That kind of thinking could one day save your job if management decides it is cost-efficient to eliminate people who need too much supervision. Here are some suggestions for creating greater job satisfaction in a large- or medium-sized organization.

Always be aware of the Big Picture. Exactly how does your position fit into the overall operations of your company? Is your position or function specifically mentioned in the company's organizational chart? Is your job necessary in a process that is important to the jobs of other workers? Can you see the direct impact of your job on the final product or income of your company? What is the history of your position? Was it created because the company wanted your particular skills and talents? What caused the new opening for your position? What happened to the last person who did your job? Were they promoted to a higher level of responsibility? And more importantly, do you have the same skills necessary for you to be promoted in the same direction?

Know how necessary your job is to the Big Picture. Does your position involve a level of responsibility that could easily be taken on by some other position? If so, begin to look for ways to increase the value and uniqueness of what you do. The more you learn about your position, your company and your industry, the more likely you will be considered indispensable.

Learn as much as you can about the positions around you, below you and above you. If it becomes necessary to downsize and you are proficient in positions in addition to your own, you are the one the company is likely to keep.

Explore ways to create a "new" position for yourself. Learning new skills, discovering new services, creating new programs or products or finding new ways to solve old problems that are relevant to your company's business can lead to a whole new set of responsibilities for you that no other employee has done in the past. You may reap a new title or even a promotion. Most organizations will be happy to reward innovative thinking in their employees. (The problem of those who are not is discussed in the section on corporate culture.)

Make these suggestions part of a continuous process. You can never let yourself "settle." That doesn't mean you should be constantly fearful for your job, but you will be ensuring a much more secure future in a large organization if you stay flexible and open to new ways to increase your value to the company.

Remember when we looked at the relationship between you and your job as similar to a love relationship? It is always in flux. However subtle the change is, it's it is up to you to manage the fluid situation. Never take your job for granted—and don't let your company take you and your position for granted, either. Find ways to make it new.

Creating Job Satisfaction in a Small Company

The majority of workers in this country are employed by small businesses, defined as less than one hundred-fifty employees. Small businesses have their own special structural difficulties. Whereas employees in large organizations usually have some insulation between themselves and the top brass, employees in small companies often have to deal directly with the president or CEO on a daily basis. These entrepreneurial types (almost always a command-person) set the tone for the entire company, dictating how things are to be done and who will take responsibility for them. And, of course, they can circumvent their own systems whenever they wish.

If you work in a small company, you may be frustrated by the seemingly arbitrary control wielded by the top person. Or, the lack of insulating management layers may allow you to work more independently and structure your own position with some freedom. Your perspective will depend upon your personality type and how you cope with the personality of the leader.

Ted was an accountant executive in a small public relations firm. The owner, Sam, was a very outgoing and forceful man who built his business on his own wits and hard work. He demanded a high level of quality, hard work and dedication from his people, as well. He seemed to prize independent thinking. But Ted found that Sam questioned every decision he made. Sam was constantly checking up on Ted to see how he handled a project. Ted began to think that most of the time Sam did not like the way the project was handled.

After receiving much verbal criticism and revision of his work, Ted finally quit making decisions and taking responsibility for his projects. He waited for Sam's input and then let his support people carry out the details. Sam's behavior sabotaged Ted's ability to work independently. Ted felt that his position in the firm was not needed.

This example is really sad; Sam hired Ted because of his attention to detail, hard work and accuracy. But Sam was frustrated because he really missed doing projects himself. He simply could not keep his hands off the projects and let his people perform their tasks. He didn't understand this until Ted quit to start his own firm, leaving Sam shocked that his employee became his competition. Sam would have been wise to simply take on a small project from time to time, to keep his hand in and keep up with changes in the field.

Understand the nature of entrepreneurs. As the above example shows, it can be difficult to work with entrepreneurs who run small businesses. If you must deal with this type of personality on a daily basis, refer to Chapter Four: *How to Love the Boss You Hate*. It helps to remember that most entrepreneurs are some combination of command-person and people-person when dealing with them (especially if you are a different personality type).

Always do your job the way you feel is best. Even though the entrepreneur may decide to change a project once you've done it, you should always do it the best way you know how from the beginning. If you try to second-guess someone else in order to do a job the way you think that person would do it, you will likely end up with a result that neither of you finds satisfactory.

You will do the best job when you approach it from your strengths and skills, not someone else's. Even if it is changed, you know that you have done your best work. And if the altered version fails, whether or not she admits it, at least the boss will know that your original recommendation may have been better.

Learn to be flexible and adaptable to almost any circumstance. In smaller businesses, things often change quickly. Because there is not a lot of bureaucracy, it is often easy for a small business to react quickly to a sudden market opportunity. That means a lot of work may be last-minute, without adequate time to prepare or go through the proper organizational channels. If you are one of the more outgoing personalities, command-persons and people-persons, you may not mind that. It may seem like an exciting challenge. But for detail-persons and support-persons—the more organized and thorough personalities—it can be exasperating. For the sake of your sanity and your stress level, you must learn to be flexible. Remind yourself that change can be good when competing for business, and that the company that tries to keep up can stay viable and offer better job-security for its employees.

In small companies, organizational systems also tend to change frequently. Sometimes they are ignored or circumvented. Because there are less layers to go through, it is easier for projects to go from start to finish without going through established channels. If you are uncomfortable in that kind of structural atmosphere, you may want to consider finding a job in a larger organization. Otherwise, adaptability is your only hope of coping.

Communicate directly and openly with your boss and co-workers. In small companies, gossip and rumors circulate quickly and tend to reach the very people they are meant to avoid. It is always best to discuss problems directly with the people concerned. If they hear it through "the grapevine," a tense situation will only get worse. Remember to approach discussions of concerns with a positive attitude. Try, "Because that job was not put through normal channels, I was unable to get the information I needed to complete it on time. Is there a way we can prevent that from happening when a job has to be done quickly?" Instead of, "You didn't get the job done and it made me late!" The key is to discuss the solution to the problem, not the behavior of an individual. Assigning blame only puts people on the defensive and does not solve the problem. Even if others in the organization put the emphasis on blaming, you can help steer them away from it by continuing to focus on the potential solutions.

Look for ways to enhance the value of your position. In the more casual structure of small companies, there is often a great deal of flexibility in job descriptions. Take every opportunity to learn more about your job and your field. Look for ways to expand your responsibilities. Look for ways you can improve the quality of the company's output. You may even create a new position for yourself. You will achieve greater satisfaction on the job when you allow yourself to stretch and grow. Your entrepreneurial boss will also look favorably on your creativity and drive (as long as you don't take too much of the spotlight away from him or her) because it enhances your value to the company.

Can you design a new program that you feel is needed by your company's customers? In your position, can you get statistics that could support a new program or product? Do you know of something specific that a competitor offers and is popular that you could put together in your company? Can you show how your company is losing long-term customers because of something that could be changed? Develop a plan, think it through and write it down with specific changes and how each step would be accomplished. Welcome support for your plan among your co-workers, especially those whose jobs would change with your plan.

Finally, remember Ted and how he gave up and formed his own company? He knew it would be successful because he could spend his time producing a product, instead of constantly reworking it, as his boss directed. If you have supporting information and a well-thought-out plan that has been disapproved, you might want to start thinking about becoming a boss yourself. If you really believe there is a market for your idea that somebody will have to provide it, that somebody could be you.

Culture: Too Political, Too Conservative or Comfortable

You might say the culture of an organization is its personality. It is determined by the relationships in the company—who talks to whom, who listens and who makes the ultimate decisions.

The larger and more bureaucratic an organization is, usually the more formal and structured its culture is. Though there are certainly exceptions, these are the companies where employees wear business suits and address their bosses as "Mr." or "Ms." People tend to follow the structural systems more closely and stick to the organizational hierarchy in communication.

Office Politics. The one thing that is missing in your company Employees Handbook is *office politics*. Usually on your first day you are given a pamphlet that gives you policy and procedures, dress codes, holidays and benefits. Perhaps it will show an organizational flow chart with your position highlighted. However, when it comes to learning the actual way this company does business—its culture or politics—you are on your own. Your information will come from others who work there and by experience. Once you have been in the organization for a while, you learn who has the real power, who is dead weight and who must be acknowledged from a political standpoint.

Priscilla worked in a multimillion-dollar corporation that produced computer software. She was in charge of new product development. Her responsibilities included evaluating or originating new ideas for marketable software products. But most of her proposals met with resistance. Priscilla soon became aware that, although she was in charge of this area, Herbert, a marketing director who was not her supervisor—or even her superior—was the "gatekeeper" for all products. The difficulty was that he was not keeping up with the new technology, and so was not really qualified to judge her work. However, Herbert had seniority and the respect of both their superiors.

Priscilla had to make a choice: she could protest the situation or she could cope with it. She decided that building a good relationship with Herbert would be a better way to handle the problem. By asking for Herbert's input, even before presenting recommendations to top management, she was able to gain his acceptance on any project she put forth. That also helped her gain approval from the ultimate decision-makers more quickly. Priscilla's acknowledgement of that unofficial authority, which helped move her projects through, was a "politically" smart move for her own career. In a year, Herbert retired, giving Priscilla free rein and allowing her to fit into the corporate culture in the eyes of top management.

Personalities. In smaller businesses, the culture is usually shaped by the personality of the company's key leader. At one direct mail company, the president dressed daily in blue jeans and a sweatshirt. He ran the company as if it were a family, with everyone being free to be comfortable in his or her own work style. When clients were to visit, a memo was passed around the day before, and everyone dressed up for it. At another small marketing firm, the president was insistent that everyone should dress professionally. Employees were even sent to seminars to learn how to present a business image. Although the company rarely had clients visit, the president was concerned that the community sees his employees going to and from work dressed appropriately (in his view) for a successful business.

The politics in small companies can be just as complicated as in large corporations, perhaps even more so. Structural systems are usually not as strictly adhered to in smaller organizations, so it is easier for idiosyncrasies to develop. Although relationships are important in big companies, they are critical in small ones, as you do not have the insulating layers of management to protect you. You may find yourself "duking it out" directly with the CEO if you do not follow the unofficial politics of getting things accepted.

Coping with the Company's Culture

How should you adapt to your company, without straying too far from your own core values? Here are some suggestions for coping with the culture of your organization. Most of them are applicable to any size company.

Adapt your personality to that of your company. Unless the culture in your company is truly intolerable, you will do best to adapt yourself to it and play by the unwritten rules. We're not talking about ethical issues here; those will be discussed later. In this case, we are talking about traditions, pecking orders, seats of power and how that power is motivated to take action.

Try to figure out how to fit in as soon as you can. That could mean something as simple as dressing the way the company prescribes. Discover how "loose" or strict the environment is. You'll also need to learn, as Priscilla did, who to involve in getting your work accepted.

Be willing to make some compromises to accomplish your own goals. You may have to be willing to accept a compromise in order to get some of your goals accomplished. If you are trying to institute a program and experiencing resistance from certain factions in the company, you may have to work out something with them. Find out what you can do for them that may facilitate their cooperation with you. Perhaps your program would eliminate something for which they are responsible. Or they may fear other changes that would affect them if your program were adopted. As long as you are flexible enough to understand other perspectives, you can generally work out a compromise that is satisfactory for everyone.

Don't forget that some people fear change of any kind. They will usually come around if they understand the program and what changes it will bring. Be as inclusive as you possibly can to get support for your plan and, in that process, be willing to change your program if you understand what it is that is causing the fear.

Be aware of destructive cultural patterns in your organization. Some organizational cultures harbor traditions that are based on destructive ideas. For example, the glass ceiling often experienced by women and minorities is an unwritten rule that says some people don't belong in the upper ranks of management. If you are encountering cultural patterns like that, you should first try to discuss them with a trusted colleague. Get an objective point of view on the problem—is this an accurate appraisal of the situation? Once you feel sure about that, it should be brought to the attention of the human resources people. If your company is unwilling to resolve or acknowledge the problem, you may want to consider leaving or even seeking outside legal counsel.

Another type of destructive cultural pattern is the addictive organization. You've heard people described as "workaholics"—he or she comes in early and stays late. They go in to the office on Sunday mornings when it is quiet and the telephones don't ring so they can "catch-up" on their work. We often see it in people in their prime work-years—their late thirties and forties. They almost become their job. And that is really the problem. A workaholic's self-image is so wrapped up in their employment that they don't spend enough of their time away from work to lead well-balanced lives.

We will talk more about this in the next chapter, but I want to spend some time on these folks when they are in key executive positions in the company and how that directs the culture of the entire organization. People who grew up in addictive families may replay their codependent behavior in the workplace. Some people may even become addicted to the organization itself.

Dave is the owner of a small financial planning company. He is a self-taught financial planner who has built up a successful business in a relatively few years. Dave is a dynamic people-person / command-person with enough drive and ambition to make up for his lack of experience. His enthusiasm for the investment world has been enough to convince some impressive clients to do business with him.

Dave has also managed to hire excellent employees who have a great deal of experience in financial planning. However, Dave's company has an incredible employee turn-over rate: in a company of ten current employees, eleven people have left or been fired in the last four years! Turnover involved everyone from the receptionist to the senior vice president. What is the problem in Dave's company?

Dave functions like an addict, though his addiction may be hard to pinpoint. It could be a need for success and attention, a need for constant excitement (or chaos, as his employees would call it), or just plain workaholism. Dave makes his employees co-dependents. He brings in last-minute business on a regular basis and demands they work overtime to meet unreasonable deadlines. Despite the expertise of the other financial planners in the company, Dave constantly makes last-minute changes in their reports and proposals.

Dave's employees scramble to clean up his messes and make his last-minute changes, time after time. Dave has never yet had to face a client and say that he could not carry out an unrealistic promise, because his employees always sacrifice themselves to make sure the promise is carried out. Why do Dave's employees protect him and pick up the pieces for him? Perhaps some of them are acting out their experiences as co-dependents in their family lives. It may seem normal to some of them to function in this manner.

If you are encountering a similar situation you should consider moving to another company when the opportunity becomes available. There is very little chance you alone can change this environment. If you choose to stay in an abusive situation, realize your self-esteem may be damaged by the effects of that abuse. You need to be aware that a co-dependant situation is escapable. You do not deserve this treatment and it really has nothing to do with you personally.

The collateral damage in these addictive environments is the worker's family, which will disintegrate for lack of attention. Many of those who left Dave's company did so for a healthier, well-balanced life. Abuse by company culture may be deceiving, because the boss seems to be working harder than you are to keep the company viable. But when you can realize that the environment of panic is deliberately created, it is time for you to move on. The choice in any stress-filled employment situation that causes real physical and emotional illness is simple. Choose your life!

Don't let yourself be too bound by your company's culture. Though it is politically smart to play by the unwritten rules and acknowledge the real seats of power, you should never let that prevent you from stretching and growing in your job. In other words, don't be afraid to test the limits of corporate culture and traditions. Maybe no one in your position has ever made a proposal to change the system or create a new product before. Don't let culture hold you back from excelling in your job. Who knows? You may start a whole new direction for your company that will benefit you both.

Ethics: A Sticky Subject

Ethics is usually defined as a set of principles of right conduct. Values are a principle, standard or quality considered worthwhile. That would seem to say ethics are principles people tend to believe are right, whereas a value may be desirable to one person—but not to someone else. Every individual has a set of internal values developed from various influences, including: parents, teachers, churches, the media and personal experience. Professed values, however, sometimes conflict with actual ethical practices. Every organization also has a set of values, which may or may not conflict with its ethical practices. For example, a company may state it values trust in its customer relationships. However, it may use questionable ethics in hiding certain charges in its billing. In such a case, the real "value" that motivates ethical behavior may be greed.

Probably no individual working for an organization today will agree with every value or ethical practice held by that organization. After all, your values and ethics are motivated by different needs and experiences than those of the company. You may think it is unethical for your employer to dock you fifteen minutes pay if you are five minutes late, because you are motivated by your own financial values. But the company is operating from rules that say you are timed in quarter hours, in order to protect its value of employee punctuality. On the other hand, maybe the company only pays you thirty cents a mile for travel when the IRS allows you thirty-four cents a mile.

Such minor differences in values are really not crucial to your comfort level with an organization. There will always be some conflicts of this nature. The larger ethical questions are much harder to dismiss. If your employer cuts corners in production, produces poor quality products, won't deliver on promises and guarantees, ignores its social or environmental responsibility, in the long run, the company will suffer financially and socially. This will undoubtedly reflect on you—whether you simply have to work in this environment or there is some sort of exposé.

Ethics are becoming an important part of long-range strategic planning, because it is good business. Many companies have written mission statements to identify their values and ethical practices for their employees. Such statements act as a guide for employees conducting business at all levels. The most effective mission statements are those that have incorporated input from everyone in the company, because they are a fair representation of the values held by all employees. Employees are much more likely to support something they have helped to create.

Here are some suggestions for evaluating the values and ethical practices of your company:

Read the company's official mission statement. If your company has a written statement, read it and analyze it carefully. What are the values underlying the statement? What does it imply for ethical conduct, particularly in the areas that affect your job? Is the statement clear, or is it vague and ambiguous? Do you notice a discrepancy between the statement and your company's ethical practices? If you can find an inconsistency in practice, so will someone else.

If you find the statement vague or incongruent with the way things actually are, ask for some feedback from other employees and your supervisor. You may want to suggest ways the statement could be updated or made to reflect current company values more accurately.

If your company has no mission statement, propose that it create one. If you feel comfortable doing so, you might try writing a draft yourself and letting your company's management revise it. Point out that a written statement will enhance the way all employees conduct the company's business. It will guide them in making decisions that affect the company's bottom line and its standing in the community. Also, point out it will be more difficult for employees to stray from the company's ethical standards if those standards are clearly spelled out.

Compare your company's values to your own. If you find significant discrepancies between your ethics and your company's, you need to analyze how important these inconsistencies are to your job satisfaction. You are the only one who can decide whether you can compromise your personal values. If it is a minor issue that relates to the employer's legitimate needs versus your personal needs, it may not be a serious problem. You will always have to compromise somewhat in this area. But a value difference resulting in an ethical conflict should be carefully evaluated. You may be jeopardizing your own reputation by staying with a company that has a serious ethical problem.

When you are unsure about an ethical question, consult your supervisor. Rather than make a decision on our own, you should consult with your supervisor if a situation occurs that is not ethically clear. If you make a decision without input from someone higher up in the company, it may turn out to be wrong. Asking for advice from a superior will help protect you from the consequences of that erroneous decision.

If you are asked to do something unethical, get your boss's sign-off. There may be times when your boss or your company asks you to do something you do not believe is ethical. If that occurs, always point out that the action is not ethical and that you would prefer not to be involved with it. You should also point out the possible damage to the company's reputation. In order to stand your ground, however, you may risk the perception that you are not a team player. It is up to you to decide what your priority is.

If you are still required to perform an unethical action, ask your boss to sign off on it so you are not held responsible. By signing-off, I mean that you get the order in writing, by way of a memo, directing you to do what you are told. You may also ask that the memo state that you are reluctant to do this. You should be particularly suspicious if the action is not part of your job description and is something that would normally be done by another worker. If that kind of thing occurs often, you should consider leaving the company. Of course, if the action is downright illegal, you are better off refusing. Resign if necessary.

You must decide for yourself how you best fit into your company's structure, culture and ethics. You may have to make some compromises along the way, but by following some of the suggestions in this chapter, you should be able to cope with whatever situations you encounter. You may even suggest some improvements to help your company be more prosperous and satisfying for its employees.

CHAPTER SEVEN

HOW TO LOVE YOURSELF

If you have a snapshot of yourself, take it out and look at it objectively. Ask yourself the following questions. Write down your answers.

1. If you met this face in a crowd, what would your impression be?

2. What is this person's attitude toward him / herself, about family, work, home and world conditions?

3. What is this person thinking? Is she / he thinking happy expansive thoughts or negative limiting thoughts?

4. What kind of worker is this person? Do they use their time and talents efficiently and profitably, or let complacency and disorder rule them?

5. Is this person tense or relaxed?

6. If this individual could modify his / her personality, what would change?

7. What are ten of this person's outstanding abilities, talents and strengths?

8. What are some of this person's underdeveloped areas?

9. What are three of this individual's personal ambitions? Explain why she / he wants to achieve them.

Now that you have answered these questions, know that your actions, feelings, behaviors and abilities are consistent with your self-image. The image you hold of yourself determines your success and happiness. Your present self-image is the product of your past experiences, attitudes and conditioning—including your ethnic, cultural or religious background, gender, identity, age, personality and physical condition. Your self-image is your mental, emotional and spiritual picture of yourself. It sets the boundaries of your accomplishments. Nothing can be accomplished that is inconsistent with it.

Are you projecting a distorted self-image to people without even realizing it? You act according to what you believe about yourself. If you believe that you cannot accomplish a certain goal, chances are you will not achieve it. Is your self-image an honest, objective representation of you and your abilities? Or are you showing people a poor self-image, representing yourself as less capable than you really are?

You may be wondering what this has to do with *How to Love the Job You Hate,* but please read this chapter carefully. Self-esteem—the estimation of your abilities and worth—has a lot to do with your relationships with co-workers and supervisors. It affects your performance on the job and your chances of being considered for promotions. After all, if you ask a boss to give you the responsibility of a $200,000 project, or supervision of twenty-five employees, and you are projecting a distorted self-image, you may not be granted your request.

Perhaps the topic of low self-esteem doesn't apply to you, but could explain the actions of a co-worker who seems discontented, hostile, complains a lot or is overly-timid. If you suspect this applies to a colleague and you are close enough to be considered an ally, encourage them to seek counseling. You may be doing them the biggest favor of their lives

Where do you get your self-image and self-esteem in the first place? Psychologists explain that your image of yourself is first formed as a reflection of what you saw mirrored in other people's reaction to you. Its primary formation takes place during the first few years of your life and comes predominantly from your parents. Other close family members also played a significant role. If you were told consistently you were smart and could achieve anything, you probably grew up believing that you could. However, if you constantly heard negative messages, those messages will be difficult to overcome when you are an adult. Are you aware you play those messages in your head, as an adult?

Were you compared to your siblings as being less smart or attractive, for example? Were you told that you were exactly the same as a relative, perhaps a parent, who was a failure? Maybe it wasn't that bad. Maybe you picked up subtle messages that were programmed in your mind.

The formation of your self-image and self-esteem doesn't rest entirely with other people, however. It also depends on your response to their reactions.

Society is full of success stories of people who came from horrible backgrounds. Carol Burnett has written and talked about her tremendous success in spite of being deserted by her parents at an early age. Oprah Winfrey was raised by her grandmother until the age of six, bounced between arguing parents and raped by a cousin. She has been able to overcome her past and help millions of people in the process. Your personality, environment, culture and other circumstances of your life will all affect your self-esteem. It will also affect your personal and professional success. A positive self-esteem can help you feel effective, productive, capable and lovable.

As we go deeper in this chapter, you will learn how the various symptoms of low self-esteem relate to the personality type of the individual.

Techniques for Building Self-esteem

Focus on your strengths. Learn how to be really good at one thing. Maybe you're a gourmet chef or a whiz with numbers. Becoming skilled in one area will help you build your self-esteem and influence other areas of your life.

Always remember to be interested in other people. One of the best ways to stop feeling sorry for yourself is to find someone who is worse off than you and help him or her. More often than not, most people will realize how blessed they are when they help someone who is less fortunate

To be successful, you need to eliminate old negative thoughts. Any Olympic winner will tell you that positive self-analysis is important. Remind yourself how capable and worthy you are. You are not the creation of an assembly line—you are unique. No one else has your fingerprints, your thoughts or your way of seeing and doing things.

Don't be afraid to take risks. You wouldn't be where you are now if you hadn't taken some risks. Who knows what you can achieve tomorrow if you take more. Try a new adventure, learn a new skill or befriend a new person. It may change your life.

Fostering positive self-esteem requires the following:

- Acceptance of strengths and weaknesses

- Encouragement

- Praise and taking pride in achievements (even little ones)

- Helping and reaching out to others for assistance and support

- Regular personal time to take care of yourself

- Respect for your own uniqueness
- Love for the special person you are becoming

Whatever your self-image, you can choose to change. It isn't easy, but it is possible. The most adverse conditioning, the worst handicap and the most crippling self-image can be overcome. I am a living example.

My high school counselor reinforced my shaky opinion of myself. She told my parents that I would never make it through college, but my natural optimism helped me thrive. I had an English teacher who loved my writing. Mr. Price helped me believe in myself when I had a difficult time with my self-esteem.

Typically, the reaction to negative personal information is either to cave in and believe it or fight. I chose to challenge that prediction of failure because that is my temperament. I became a high achiever, determined to show those adults that they were wrong about me. In just five years, I had both a Bachelor and a Masters degree from Ohio State University, and I even finished my Masters with a 4.0 average. However, it still took me years beyond college to learn that I didn't have to perform in order to be accepted. I still thought I needed straight A's, have fabulous job offers, a perfect marriage and accolades to be lovable. Now I know I am okay just the way I am.

Is Work Your Source of Identity?

Society reinforces the idea that our work determines our worth. What has traditionally been the first question asked of a man in social conversation? "What do you do for a living?" If he doesn't have a good answer, society wonders what is wrong with him. Women are now experiencing the same problem. If she chooses to stay home and care for her children, she is somehow thought to be inferior to the woman who works outside the home.

During a recent speaking engagement, I was approached by Josh, one of the key people with his company. He told me that in one year he would be retiring. In his entire life, he had never considered who he was outside of his job. He was afraid. He didn't know what he was going to do with his life. Josh is not alone. Millions of men and women define themselves solely by their employment. If your work is unfulfilling or boring, your life becomes that way, as well.

We sometimes feel that if we *are* our jobs, it speaks volumes about who we are and how we are trying to live. It doesn't. It is just a job. Our work allows us to get our needs met. It's a shame that nobody ever figured out a way for us to ask each other, "Who are you and what do you do to support the people and things you love?"

A person with a positive self-image realizes that work is an important part of his or her life, but it isn't everything. It may seem obvious that the better you feel about yourself, the better you will perform, but in fact it isn't. The key is to cultivate a stable self-image that can handle the bad days without letting self-esteem plummet when failure occurs.

How Your Self-Image Affects Your Job

People with low self-esteem tend to suffer from higher levels of physical and emotional stress, resulting in higher absentee rates on the job. How workers handle stress is a major concern in the workplace. Stress has become nothing less than a national epidemic.

Marcia Holmes, a fitness and wellness educator, who counsels organizations on how to reduce stress in the workplace, believes there is a direct correlation between stress and self-esteem. The higher your stress level, the more out of control you feel; the more your self-esteem is affected. In turn your productivity is affected.

When a person is deeply insecure because they suffer from low self-esteem, he or she may feel jealousy and envy. They may feel so badly about themselves that they can't stand to see someone else get something they secretly think they deserve. They measure their worth in comparison to what others have or don't have. If that situation describes you, you are on the wrong track.

Recognizing Low Self-Esteem in the Workplace

People often ask how to recognize the beginning signs of an ailing self-esteem. How do you know when your self-esteem is low enough to be a serious problem? One of the most obvious symptoms is expecting to fail.

Donald is an example of a person who was programmed to fail. His father was not patient in his parenting of Donald and often became exasperated with his young son. Donald's mother offered more sympathy and attention when her son failed. Together, Donald's parents reinforced a cycle of failure that convinced Donald, early in life, that he was incompetent at everything he tried to do. As his father supervised a task and became exasperated, Donald got sympathy and attention for his weaknesses. Later in life, his wife's attempts at encouragement were fruitless, even meeting with stubborn resistance. Donald's pattern was so ingrained in his thinking that any praise was suspect. He came to resent his wife for not waiting to give him sympathy and attention when he failed—and fail he would, to get what was familiar. Rather than take a risk to try to achieve, Donald found comfort and safety in his identity as a failure.

Donald always loved history and knew fascinating stories about happenings in time as he took his family on vacations to visit historic sites. His wife tried to encourage him to go to night school to become a history teacher. But Donald's negative messages kept playing in his mind. He was sure he could never get through college. If by some miracle he did, he would be an awful teacher who would not be heard by students. Instead, Donald got a job in a factory, repeating simple routine tasks over and over. He never had to take a risk or learn something new. For more than forty years Donald made good wages. When he retired, he talked of how he hated his job. He had been a "good provider" and always financially secure—but he was miserable.

The other side of the underachiever syndrome is the overachiever, who does everything for the purpose of receiving approval and bolstering a fragile self-esteem. Ruth was driven to achieve straight A's in school because she didn't believe she was acceptable if she achieved anything less. Believing the more she achieved, the better she would feel about herself, she sacrificed her health and personal life to her workaholic drive. But Ruth discovered that no matter how well she did something, someone else could do it better. Whenever she reached a goal, there was yet another one to reach. And no matter how far up the ladder she climbed, someone else was always closer to the top. Ruth finally realized that she could never be "the best" because there would always be someone better. This is a story of success because Ruth finally realized that instead of worrying others might outdo her, she could revel in her achievements.

Low self-esteem tends to project the resulting poor self-image to others. How do others see Donald? Exactly as he sees himself: a self-perpetuating failure. People saw Ruth as a perfectionist who could never be satisfied in herself or the attempts of colleagues. Her subordinates knew not to try.

While a common symptom of low self-esteem is a lack of confidence, what most people don't realize is that overconfidence and aggressiveness can also be symptoms of low self-esteem. People who are considered braggarts may be constantly telling everyone how great they are because they really fear they are not. A need to prove superiority, exercise inordinate control over others or receive credit for even the minutest involvement in projects is often the symptom of a severe inferiority complex.

A healthy self-image is balanced with a high amount of self-esteem for one's own abilities, paired with acknowledgment of your worth as an individual.

One must also have enough objectivity to realistically recognize weaknesses and under-developed areas. In other words, you are superior in some things, equal in others and inferior in others. Compared to every other person in the world, you are just right for you.

First Aid for Self-esteem

How do you begin to feel better about yourself? There are many different methods for enhancing self-esteem and thus, creating a more realistic self-image. It can be a long, hard process, but it can be done.

As I have suggested earlier, if you have a serious problem, you should never feel ashamed to seek professional counseling. Most people wouldn't hesitate to consult a professional for a medical problem. Emotional concerns can be just as critical and life-threatening as any disease, so it is just as important to take positive action and seek help.

The following suggestions are by no means the definitive method for boosting self-esteem, but they are things you can begin to do immediately that will start the process of healing.

Get in touch with your feelings. Remember in the Seventies and early Eighties when people were telling each other to "get in touch with their feelings?" What once was hip cliché turned out to be a valid need.

A lot of people have learned to wear emotional masks to hide their real personality. Most do this to protect themselves from rejection. The logic is if someone doesn't like the façade, at least he or she is not disapproving of the real person under it. The thinking is people will like the false front better than their real selves. The sad reality of this tactic is they are most often rejected because other people don't like the mask itself. They sense something phony and pull away.

If a feeling is too painful or difficult to face, everyone has a way to hide it, either consciously or unconsciously. If you are ever going to begin appreciating the person you are, however, you have to know your true self. You must learn to recognize reality and take responsibility for it without resorting to denials, defense mechanisms or other inappropriate coping methods. These include creating that façade, using alcohol, drugs, or obsessions for an escape. Any of these things can be used to deny reality in an attempt to try to protect yourself from taking responsibility for who and what you are.

Be Yourself. One of the greatest challenges in life is knowing who you really are. It may seem very simple, but it offers profound results. First, try taking off the mask with people you are closest to and trust the most. Then try it with others. After all, you are unique. There is no one else in the world exactly like you, so why not be you? That doesn't mean that there aren't some things you may want to change about yourself. There's nothing wrong with wanting to improve yourself and work on your faults.

Accept your limitations. If you are over thirty, your chances of qualifying for the next U.S. Olympic swim team or winning the Heisman trophy are slim. There are some things you cannot do, but that doesn't invalidate you as a person. Identify your shortcomings. If you can change them, do. If you can't, balance these limitations with your strengths—or develop new positives.

Forgive yourself. If you make a mistake, allow yourself enough time to learn from it, so it won't happen again. Be as understanding with yourself as you would with another person who made an honest mistake. Wouldn't you say something like, "Don't get upset, I will help you fix the problem," or "Well, now we know what *not* to do," and even, "You know, I made that mistake myself when I first worked here." You would never say, "I can't imagine how you could be so stupid as to have made that mistake" or "Only a complete idiot would do that."

Often times, our goof-ups can cause us to feel guilty. But this feeling can be so all-consuming that it actually prevents you from taking responsibility for the mistake—you don't dare admit it. Let go of the guilt. Do what you can to rectify the situation honestly. Apologize if that is what is called for. Learn from the situation and move on.

Look for sources of emotional support. Who listens to you, loves and appreciation you? Who challenges you to be *you* more fully? Other people can provide support in this, as you can for others who may need it.

Take care of yourself. You need to remember that your health must come first or you can't do anything else for anyone. You can begin to uplift your self-esteem by focusing on your health. Take time to eat well and get physical exercise. Lay off the caffeine and sugar. What about your sleeping habits? Do you get enough restful sleep each night? Is your entire weekend taken up by falling into bed on Friday and pretty much staying there until Monday morning?

Taking care of yourself also includes projecting a healthy self-image to others. It may not seem fair, but people do size you up and judge you by the way you look. Your personal grooming habits definitely project how you feel about yourself. If you look like you don't take care of yourself, with a sloppy and unhealthy appearance, others won't think highly of you because you don't project confidence.

Treat yourself with respect. We've talked quite a bit about treating others as you would like to be treated. But you also need to treat *yourself* well. If you think you don't deserve the best, that you're not worthy of respect or love, you are not likely to think anyone deserves it or is worthy either. Why be ruled by cynicism, disillusionment and resentment? Remember that you are a human being. Treat yourself like a valid person, according yourself the same dignity, respect and care that all human beings deserve. That doesn't mean that you put your needs above all others all the time—that is selfishness. You need to take care of yourself, keeping yourself healthy, both physically and mentally.

Avoid co-dependency. Being co-dependent means that you ignore your own needs and put the needs of another in front of your own. When people are really co-dependent, they can lose their entire sense of self.

An example of co-dependency is the boss who takes advantage of you and others. If you work for a supervisor who demands more and more from you, forces you to work overtime and take on more projects than you can really handle, you must wake up and identify the problem. You need to stop allowing people to force you into doing more than you can manage.

When you change your self-esteem for the better, others will show respect for your positive self-image. You will get the confidence to say no when it is necessary. Those who are used to "dumping" on you will be a bit taken aback if you set new boundaries on how much you can take on for others. They will get over it—or if they don't, you need to move on. *You* decide when your plate is full, when you are doing all you possibly can for others and stick to it. Your life depends on it.

Get involved. You need people and they need you. Don't hide because you feel you have nothing worth contributing. Get involved with co-workers you don't usually work around. Start a new project, take a class, learn something new, befriend a different co-worker and start a social group or book club. Invite colleagues to your home. You need to invest in your job, just as your employer has invested in you. Becoming more involved in your job and other areas of your life will pay off with dividends for your self-esteem.

Consciously visualize a good self-image. Mentally picture how you want your life to be. Concentrate on the positive changes you want to make in your life. To boost your self-image, you need to alter the way you think about yourself. Remind yourself of the good qualities that you would like to strengthen. Observe the characteristics of people you admire. Ask friends and confidants how they overcame their own fears. The image you put into your mind today will be the image you project tomorrow.

Don't compare yourself to others. No one's life is as perfect as it looks, so don't try to model yourself exactly on another's. You have no idea what problems they are working on each day. Remember you are only seeing the self-image they choose to project.

The key is to accept your differences. It's okay to have different levels of experience, talent or intelligence than your co-workers. You and your colleagues are all at different stages in your lives and it takes different workers to form a team. Every person is unique and you have some talent, experience or willingness to bring to the table, even if it is simply a fresh observation on the problem.

There is a story about a salesman and a janitor at the AlkaSelzer Company. The sales manager, Vic, was working late one night. He was worried about the direction of the product. Somehow he had to increase sales. The janitor, Al, asked Vic why he was working so late on a Friday night. Al explained his dilemma. The janitor asked what the directions on the box said. Al read them aloud: Take one tablet, plop, plop, fizz, fizz, and so on.

Al asked, "Does it hurt to take more than one tablet at a time?"

Vic checked his notes. No, it did not. So, at Al's suggestion, Vic changed the directions from "take one" to "take two." Almost overnight, sales doubled.

Sometimes the people who we least suspect have the most to offer.

Verbalize good self-esteem. When having an internal dialog with yourself, always keep it positive. Your energy is much better spent in projecting a genuinely positive attitude, and that is best accomplished when you feel positive toward yourself and others. Keep your self-evaluation positive and you'll find that it makes others feel more positive toward you.

Your fears and beliefs can have a lot of power over your life. They are not reality; they are only ideas that can have positive or negative impacts on your attitudes and behavior. These beliefs come from your past programming—some of which has had a good influence, but some has distorted your self-image. Your task now is to work on reversing the effects of the bad programming.

Remember that everything you say to yourself and to others is being recorded in your head, so try to make it as positive and nurturing as you can. Occasionally, constructive criticism is necessary. Whether the constructive criticism is for yourself or for another, direct the remarks to the action and not the person. Couch it as a learning experience for future use.

Accept whatever is valid in both criticism and compliments. People with low self-esteem have a hard time accepting either compliments or criticism. They take criticism too much to heart and dwell on it. They often refuse to believe a compliment. When you receive criticism, examine it. Accept the valid part of it that you can learn from. Throw the rest out. When you receive a compliment, it's a gift! Appreciate it. Unless the compliment is exaggerated empty flattery, accept it as truth. Be gracious to the person who gave it to you. Allow yourself to feel good about it.

Make a think / thank list. List all of your blessings, all of the good things that you are thankful for about yourself and your life. It helps to realize there are things to appreciate.

Write down your good qualities, accomplishments and talents. Don't leave anything out. Once you get that list going, use it to help reshape your self-image. Keep all the positive things in your life on this list, including family, friends, work and home.

Now list your personal and professional ambitions. Be as specific as possible. Figure out where you are on the road to making those goals a reality.

When I worked with a group of displaced homemakers—women who had raised their families and were just starting back to school in midlife—I asked them to cut out pictures from magazines. These had to be of something they wanted to buy with their own wages. I told them to put those pictures up on their bedroom wall. Every morning when they climbed out of bed, they would be reminded of why they needed to get going. Everything they did during the day would eventually lead to something they really wanted. I also asked them to share it with their families. That way, the picture would help the family members cheer on their wife / mother as they strove to reach their goal.

The pictures were as different as the women were, and there were many surprises. One was of a sleek modern kitchen because the woman wanted to finish college and remodel her home. Another had a picture of a tropical island getaway resort where she would take her husband for a second honeymoon. These goals were long term. The women had years of college ahead of them before they would earn wages, but they jumped on the exercise, making me guess that they all had longed for these dreams for quite sometime.

The think / thank list gives you the opportunity to see where you've come from: the hurdles you had to jump over, the negative experiences you had to get past. Use the list to remind yourself of the goals you have accomplished and the things that already good in your life. That will help you maintain a positive outlook and make new plans for the future.

What Is "Reaching Your Potential?"

The benefit of repaired and strengthened self-esteem is the ability to reach your potential—to be the best you can be. Some people settle for less, like the factory worker who could have been a history teacher. Some may fear failure, like he did, and others will fear success. They are comfortable with what they have now in terms of a job or relationship. They fear delving into the unknown, which might be worse. Life is a risk and none of us would be where we are now if we hadn't taken some risks. We will never get to be where we want to be tomorrow if we don't take some more. When you have good self-esteem, those risks won't seem half as scary. You'll have the confidence you need to tackle anything.

CHAPTER EIGHT
HOW TO LOVE THE STRESS YOU HATE

Stress in itself is not bad. It can be positive or negative, stimulating or debilitating. Stress is simply the mental and physical tension that occurs when you do something other than stand, sit or lie still. No stress means you are asleep, unconscious or dead! Some stress is necessary to keep you active and motivated.

Though Americans may have a better balance of work, family and leisure time, we are not coping with negative stress very well. The abuse of alcohol and drugs to cope with the mental, emotional and physical (pain) effects of stress costs the United States more than one hundred billion dollars a year in increased medical expenses, worker's compensation claims, lost time and productivity. In this chapter we will examine responses to stress, and healthy, effective ways to cope.

My research indicates stress is the biggest health and benefit concern affecting the workplace. High stress is insidious, as there is no way of preventing burnout levels of stress in all employees because everyone deals with it differently. When an employee becomes overstressed, employers must accommodate that person's work-related problems (situations ranging from poor productivity to chronic tardiness to addiction), related medical and / or psychotherapy expenses and the effect that person has on his or her co-workers' stress levels. A stressful environment in the workplace almost always contributes to high employee turnover rates. Stress is the most expensive personnel cost employers face. Remember the crisis shelter director who said that her employees had a way of weeding themselves out? Even if that is a given, high employee turnover is very expensive for the employer and devastating to the employees who lose confidence in their ability to work. Just as skills training is part of taking care of the workers, employers must actively manage stress levels in the work environment by budgeting for on-going *self-care training*. If the company does not provide this, it is up to you, the worker, to take care of yourself and avoid high levels of stress at your job.

Why Are We So Vulnerable to Stress Today?

Dealing with the kind of constant upheaval one finds in life today creates a lot of stress. Workers are more vulnerable to stress than previous generations because they have fewer support systems. Lifestyles have altered tremendously in the last fifty years. Marriage to one partner over a lifetime is no longer the norm. Once, large extended families were involved with all of its members, helping each other in times of crisis. Now most families are scattered all over the country, if not the world. Divorce and remarriage are much more prevalent, resulting in more single-parent households and whole new family structures. While religion is still part of people's lives, it used to be a cornerstone of a person's life. Before the 1970s, workers labored for the same organization for thirty or forty years. Now employees are changing jobs an average of four or five times during their work life.

Without stability and traditional methods of support, workers are suffering greater effects of stress. Economic boom and bust cycles inspire un-certainty and fear in workers with no clear support system to fall back on. For many, just the thought of losing one's job leaves them crippled with depression or stress-related physical illness.

Recognizing the Need for Stress Management

Many companies are implementing stress management programs be-cause of the many links between health problems and stress. The treatment for these illnesses and injuries has skyrocketed as healthcare costs have increased. Some larger companies have employee assistance or wellness programs. Many smaller organizations are following suit. Businesses are beginning to realize that prevention is often much more cost-efficient than necessary cures. For example, it makes sense to pay for an addiction recovery program before a substance abus-ing employee needs treatment or gets in trouble with the law. Promoting stress-relieving fitness programs is more cost effective than letting an overworked, overstressed employee become so ill he needs a $50,000 heart bypass operation.

If your company has a wellness or employee assistance programs, here is the kind of help you may be able to get:

- Literature should be made available to employees which states how the program operates. There should be a clearly stated policy describing how the company will help with particular problems or needs.

- Often a short-term counseling service is available during off-hours at no charge to the employee. This may take the form of a twenty-four-hour help line or a contracted service you can visit locally.

- Some type of fitness or wellness program is usually included with exercise or aerobics classes, free or reduced cost use of health club facilities or an incentive program that rewards you for fitness activities you do on your own.

Don't Let Fear Stop You. I have a friend whose brother Al has worked for a city for fifteen years. Some time ago he got into trouble when, due to budget constraints, there was a hiring freeze. He and many of his fellow employees worked long over-time hours to get all the work done.

After three years, the Mayor was alarmed at estimates that as many as 70 percent of municipal employees could have substance abuse problems resulting from work-related stress. He quietly circulated an in-office memo saying that any of the three thousand municipal employees would receive free medical care and a ninety-day substance abuse recovery program if they reported their problem to their personnel officer during the amnesty period. Only two employees took advantage of the offer of help—Al was one of them.

Of course, Al was afraid to admit he had a problem with illegal substances, but it was his only hope of keeping his job and getting help for his expensive addiction at the same time. He remembers the personnel officer asking, "Are you here to save your job and your retirement?" He was grateful for the compassion. As a result of this medical care, Al also found out he had dangerously high blood pressure. His act of courage was a double lifesaver for him.

After the amnesty period, there were news leaks exposing addicted municipal employees. Many people lost their jobs, their retirement and their health. Some experienced financial and family ruin. But my friend reports Al is healthy and sober. He accepts over-time hours only when he feels comfortable with it. He has set realistic boundaries at work and is back to feeling good about his job and his life. Al has never experienced anything but support from his supervisors for his recovery program. His health plan continues to cover follow-up counseling as needed.

Don't hesitate to take advantage of such a program if it is available to you. If your organization does not have one, you may want to propose the possibility be investigated. Chapter Thirteen: *Addressing Your Employees Needs,* will provide you with some information about the cost benefits for your company that you can show to your management people.

How You Can Recognize Your Stress Level

Stress usually begins with a feeling of being challenged or threatened. Your brain sends signals to certain glands, which in turn send out chemical signals, and stress hormones pour into your blood stream. You feel the effects immediately. Your heart rate goes up, your blood pressure increases, your pupils dilate, your blood volume and sodium levels increase. More blood is directed to your muscles and liver for quick energy. Normally, after the threat is over, your body automatically returns to normal. But if you are exposed to stress repeatedly, or if it continues without a break for long periods of time, your body can no longer recover. You will begin to experience physical symptoms such as headaches, backaches and so on.

As mentioned earlier, headaches, backaches, stomach problems, over-susceptibility to colds and sinus infections are common warning signs that your stress level is too high. However, many people do not realize that those symptoms are due to stress. Of course, they can be symptoms of some other physical ailment—but all too often they are telling you that there is too much unrelieved stress in your life. Knowing your own personality and physical condition will help you determine how much stress you can manage adequately before you decide you need to change your stressful environment or seek some professional help.

Take the following quiz to see if your body is trying to tell you something. This test is not intended as a scientific diagnosis in any way, but merely a guide to the level of stress you are currently experiencing.

On a piece of paper, write out each of these symptoms. Next to each respond with the following numbers: 3-Frequently; 2-Occasionally; 1-Rarely / Never

Are you experiencing any of the following?

- Head, neck or backaches

- Fatigue or exhaustion

- Poor short-term memory

- Chest pains or shortness of breath

- Anxiety or irritability

- Indigestion or stomach pains

- Difficulty sleeping

- Inability to relax

- Rushed or skipped meals

- Little or no exercise

- Increase or decrease in appetite

- Increased mistakes or accidents

- Lack of stamina

Scoring: A score of 15 or lower indicates you have a low degree of stress in your life. You are handling a stressful environment with little or no negative impact on your life. A result of 16-26 means you have an average amount of stress. You handle stress in a healthy manner. A tally of 27 or higher means that your stress level is particularly high. A stressful environment is having a negative impact on your life. You need to make some changes.

If your score is high, this does not mean you have too much stress at work, or that your personal life is too stressful. One area of your life could be impacting on the other, or you may be experiencing moderate levels of stress in two areas of your life. Stress is cumulative. You can also be a person who never learned to handle stress in a healthy manner.

Just remember that you can control the impact that stress has on your well-being as long as you are aware of it. Some people have even learned to make a moderate level of stress their motivation to reach their optimal potential. So can you.

Different Personality Types Can Handle Different Stress Levels

We've discussed people- and command-person types—these outgoing, dynamic and energetic types can handle a somewhat higher stress level than the calmer, more introverted detail- and support-person types. However, the less positive personality attributes of people- and command-persons—aggression, a need to compete and workaholism—can also contribute to an increased risk of heart attacks. Detail- and support-persons tend to turn their stress inward, frequently becoming cautious hypochondriacs or causing themselves physical and psychological harm by holding their negative feelings inside.

These are only tendencies, of course, and they will be affected by an individual's heredity and current physical condition. Knowing these traits may help you understand why you are or are not able to tolerate certain levels of stress.

How You Can Cope with Your Stress Level—Physically

Medical research shows that exercising and being aerobically fit can temper the effects of stress. It limits the rise in stress hormones and therefore controls the amount your heart rate will escalate during stress. Quick jumps in heart rate have been linked to heart attacks, particularly for people- and command-persons, so being in good condition can save your life. Because a fit body doesn't release as much stress hormone into your system, your system can also return to normal more quickly after a stress response.

Regular physical exercise also releases endorphins into your system. Endorphins are a biochemical that give you a natural high, which is what runners often experience. This chemical makes you feel good, helps to stabilize the effect of stress hormones and minimizes pain. To get the maximum benefit from endorphins, it is necessary to exercise regularly. There is a point of overdoing, however. Above a certain intensity, exercise stimulates the same mechanism as stress, and high levels of cortisol can be permanently activated. Chronically elevated levels of cortisol can cause suppression of the immune system, depression and other serious problems.

People- and command-personalities sometimes become actual stress addicts. I mentioned earlier that these people, sometimes referred to as adrenaline junkies, can wreck havoc for everyone at work. They can't stop their harried lifestyles because they are hooked on the rush of adrenaline they get from their body's stress response. Though some people- and command-personalities may enjoy this behavior, they are not doing their bodies any favors. Nor are the detail- and support-co-workers whose stress is increased by the demands of this harried work environment.

One interesting method of coping with stress is to cry. It has been found tears contain high levels of stress hormones, indicating that crying is a way of releasing excess hormones from the body. Women, on the whole, tend to suffer from stress less than men do, though that is changing in today's workforce. The greater societal acceptance of women's crying may play a big part in helping them cope with stress.

Some methods of coping with stress, such as smoking, drinking alcohol or caffeine and eating foods high in sugar, salt or fat, actually increase stress, rather than relieve it. Skipping meals and sacrificing sleep also aggravate and add to stressful conditions. Keeping yourself in the best possible physical condition will help reduce the effects of your body's stress response and lessen the physical damage that excessive or chronic stress can cause.

Your attitude plays a large role in how effective exercise is in keeping you in shape and lowering your stress level. If you exercise primarily because you think you should, you'll probably add more stress to your life. Try to find some type of exercise you enjoy doing. Whether you choose to play a competitive sport, walk with your spouse or a friend, dance or romp in the grass with your kids, make it a fun part of your life and it will prove to be much more beneficial. If time is an issue (and time is always an issue for workers, today) go back to Chapter Two: *How to Fall Back in Love With Your Job* and review some of the suggestions for changing your workday to include physical activity. Instead of eating a bag of chips at your desk, you could have a healthy getaway, complete with some fun activity, a very healthy meal and a refreshing shower in the middle of the day. You would escape the tensions of the workplace and it wouldn't cut into your personal time off with your family. You could even start a trend with this and find yourself part of a crowd of co-workers heading for the most popular exercise class. If you have one of those "crazy-making bosses" who is hooked on the adrenaline rush, go to her or him with a few co-workers for support and ask to have a little longer for lunch. These people- or command-personalities are almost always aware of their lifestyle and most likely won't be offended by your need for stress relief. If you couch it as a benefit for him or her—in that employees could start the afternoon as fresh as the beginning of the workday—it should be well-received. Remember to use the "I" or "We" message, instead of blaming the need for stress relief on the boss. Try saying: "We don't have your incredible energy all day long, and could use a healthy boost around noon to keep up with you."

Sleep is an important component in stress management. Not everyone needs eight hours, but no one can function properly on two or three hours sleep either. You can't handle stress on a few hours of sack time. In an emergency, you may be able to get away with just a couple of hours, but meeting a regular deadline at work is not an emergency. Frequently, people- and command-persons think sleep is a waste of time, but eventually they will feel the consequences in increased physical symptoms of high stress.

Diet is also very important in controlling stress. Excessive sugar, salt, fat and caffeine have helped to put one out of every two Americans at risk for coronary disease. Heart disease is still the number one killer in the United States, and coronary bypass surgery claims more healthcare dollars than any other operation, costing more than five billion dollars annually. A diet rich in complex carbohydrates, such as whole grain cereals, breads and pasta, combined with protein and dairy products which slow down sugar absorption, will give you the steady energy supply you need in stress management. Eat when you are relaxed and don't skip meals.

Quick and Easy Physical Stress Reducers

If you work in an office, you undoubtedly sit too much and move too little. Try some exercises that gently stretch your muscles to keep you limber, relieve tension, prevent knots and spasms. This type of exercise is a good complement to brisk walking, bicycling or other aerobic exercises, and you can do it almost anywhere, anytime.

When you feel the physical effects of stress at work, try:

- Deep breathing control. Slow down! Take deeper breaths.

- Progressive muscle relaxation. Alternately tense and relax groups of muscles.

- Take a walk—take the stairs.

Advanced Stress Reducers

- Massage therapy. If you can't afford a masseuse, check out a massage school—it's affordable.

- Self-help groups.

- Meditation, yoga, Tai Chi.

- Laugh, laugh and laugh some more—it feels great!

How You Can Cope with Your Stress Level—Mental and Emotional Effects

Remember the last time your boss snarled at you that you should have known about something in a report you never even received? He might have been reacting to something that caused him stress. Just as physical senses are heightened and adrenaline flow is increased under stress, mental processes also work faster than normal. In fact, long after the physical symptoms of stress have ceased, a person may still be experiencing mental and emotional symptoms such as worry, anxiety, anger and depression. These reactions can spawn unexpected outbursts like the one from your boss.

If something upsetting occurs at work, do you continue to mull over the future consequences of the incident after you get home? Do you worry that it might happen again? Do you feel anxious about what the implications may be for you and your job? Do you get angry that whatever happened might jeopardize your position or job? Or do you let yourself slide into a depression because you think you have no control over the matter? All of these responses are the mental and emotional symptoms of stress. Your reaction depends on your personality type, level of experience and maturity. The most important thing to remember is that how you cope with these feelings determines how seriously they will affect your job performance and your life.

The Japanese offer one of the best examples of stress responses from cultural work experiences. As a society, they believe in a very strict work ethic that demands a lot of each worker. This resulted in success in the global marketplace.

Japanese executives have been noted for their drive to produce and their personal disgrace for failure. Many cite a sense of terrible guilt if they take time off for a holiday or illness. They fear losing favor with their bosses. Most Japanese work a seventy-two hour workweek.

And what is the cost of all this dedication? Job-related stress has produced an alarming increase in alcoholism, mental breakdowns, suicides and family abandonment in the last two decades. Add to that the recent economic downturns that have changed the corporate culture of the country—for instance: the concept of a "job for life" has disappeared—creating yet more stress.

This is a case where a nation is experiencing an epidemic of work-related stress, but has no appropriate way to cope with it. In polls, Japanese workers express major dissatisfaction with the system, which is surprising in light of the Japanese philosophy of accepting sacrifice and foregoing personal well-being for the good of the country. Comparisons of American and Japanese feelings about their lives consistently show that the Japanese are far less satisfied with their family life, leisure time and general quality of life than Americans.

How Does Your Personality Type Handle Mental and Emotional Stress?

People- and command-persons are generally optimistic and resilient, not allowing setbacks to slow them down. They can usually handle a lot of stress without falling apart. They actually seem to thrive on pressure, but they also tend to be "hot reactors"—flying off the handle and openly expressing their impatience, displeasure and anger. Because they are ambitious go-getters, they often put in long hours and ignore their physical limitations, as well as their emotional capability, to handle stress. You might say people- and command-persons think they are invulnerable—or at least behave as if they do.

In comparison, detail- and support-persons tend to be cautious and methodical in their approach to tasks. They are more easily discouraged by setbacks—or they will approach a similar project more cautiously in the future. Detail- and support-persons often suffer high stress or anxiety when they are not given enough time to accomplish a task properly. They express their feelings reluctantly and tend to hold resentment or anger inside. This can make them candidates for physical illness. The emotional pressure has to come out somewhere, and it will likely attack the most vulnerable physical area of the detail- and support-persons.

Your individuality will affect all of these tendencies. As discussed before, you may be a combination of two types, but one is probably more dominant than the other. It can be helpful to recognize these tendencies in yourself and your coworkers, especially when you must deal with the stress they cause.

Stress and Company Culture

Another attitude that can affect these tendencies is the company culture. Written or unwritten policies in the workplace will dictate how much a stressful work environment will be tolerated. If the "deadline mentality" rules the office, the detail- and support-persons in the office are in for a rough time unless the pressure is managed effectively. I know of several high-stress offices that have groups of detail- and support-persons (usually in accounting) These people cannot tolerate the distraction of a stressful environment. The best solution is to give detail- and support-persons an office by themselves where they are as isolated as they want to be during working hours. In one case the management office was moved off-site. Care was taken, however, to include those employees in weekly staff meetings, company events and lunch hour activities.

Take control of your stress. Understanding your stress response is the key to changing it. You can learn to rethink old emotional habits. Consider the alternatives at hand and find a way to make the best of the circumstances. Find a way to release your anger without offending or hurting others. Don't just suffer in silence. In the end it will do you more harm than good.

The best attitude toward stress is summed up in the well-known *Serenity Prayer,* most often used by Alcoholics Anonymous:

God, grant me the grace to accept with serenity the things I cannot change, the courage to change the things I can, and the wisdom to know the difference.

Learn to laugh—loud and hard. You'll recall Dave, the financial planner who was such a terror: demanding his workers complete work before unrealistic deadlines; making unreasonable promises to the clients; requiring his employees clean up *his* mistakes. All this resulted in very high employee turnover. When I asked one of Dave's employees about working in the chaos, he said, "It can be a good place to work if you have a great sense of humor. Instead of getting upset, those of us who continued to work here have learned to stick together and laugh a lot—and Dave knows it. We call him the "Drama King" because he seems to thrive on it. We pick our battles and draw the line—if we all agree that something is unreasonable. But we make very good money here. This job is not for everyone. We remind each other constantly to leave the pressure at our desks and go home, on time, every day."

What Happens When Mental or Emotional Stress is Not Properly Managed?

An overload of stress usually shows up in symptoms such as chronic fatigue, withdrawal from co-workers, family and friends, decline in work performance and an increased need for escape activities. Those symptoms can also be a sign of a much more severe reaction to stress overload called burnout. Whereas stressed-out people may be *too* involved in their work, burned-out people no longer feel involved with theirs. According to psychologists, burnout occurs when the pressures and conflicts outnumber the emotional rewards of a job. Working under highly stressful conditions too long without adequate coping methods can create a feeling of being out of control and without purpose, or a sense of futility. In other words, you give up.

Burnout is also the result of unrealistic expectations imposed either by the employee, the boss or a company. Employers who constantly point out problems in employees' work—without giving praise for accomplishments—are setting employees up for eventual burnout. Feelings of helplessness and hopelessness kill motivation. That is where burnout differs from stress. People who are simply stressed out can still be highly motivated. Burned-out employees will either leave or become physically or emotionally ill.

Another serious consequence of unmanaged, unrelenting stress is depression. A person may go through a cycle that begins with symptoms of excess stress, then progresses to eventual burnout and finally, this becomes a serious depression. Or, a person may slip into depression at the first signs of excessive stress. It depends on the individual's personality, outlook on life, physical condition and demands from other areas of his or her life.

Almost everyone gets short periods of depression. It is normal to experience the blues following a distressing event or loss. But when depression persists for weeks or months, interfering with relationships, family life, work or even physical health, it may be what psychologists call clinical depression. This is caused by a depletion of a biochemical in the brain. The condition exhibits many of the symptoms of excessive stress and burnout such as irritability, fatigue, headaches, backaches, digestive problems and a feeling of hopelessness. You may notice sleep and appetite disturbances; emotional instability can include crying spells.

Clinical depression requires professional counseling and medical treatment. As many as fifteen million Americans may be experiencing clinical depression without realizing it. Left untreated, depression can lead to significant health problems.

It is important to note that clinical depression is a medical problem and must be treated by a physician. Many employee health plans do not include mental or emotional counseling, so workers erroneously believe they are not covered under their benefits. They avoid treatment, thinking they cannot afford help, hoping it will just go away. Nothing matters as much as one's health. It is important to seek treatment. Arrangements can be made with the doctor's office to pay for the services later, if, in fact, insurance doesn't cover. In many cases, your company benefit person can guide you about your benefits.

Are You At-Risk for Burnout or Depression?

The simple answer is yes. Everybody is at risk for burnout or depression, especially when you are doing more work with fewer resources. It is the wise person who keeps an eye on their stress level.

This brief quiz will help you determine whether or not you should be concerned about the possibility of burnout or depression and your current risk. Only a doctor can determine the diagnosis for your symptoms.

On a piece of paper, write out each of these symptoms. Next to each respond with the following numbers: 3-Frequently; 2-Occasionally; 1-Rarely / Never.

In the last two weeks, have you been:

- Uninterested in things you used to enjoy

- Experiencing wide mood swings

- Feeling irritable and anxious

- Feeling your life is out of control

- Overwhelmed by everyday affairs and trivial problems

- Feeling useless and unneeded

- Difficulty sleeping

- Decrease or increase in appetite

- Feeling tired with little energy for no apparent reason

- Experiencing unexplained physical ailments (headaches, indigestion, backaches, rapid heartbeat)

- Loss of concentration or ability to concentrate

- Crying frequently over small things

Scoring: below 18 = low risk; 18-23 = moderate risk; over 23 = high risk.

Your score may help you decide on a life change you've been mulling over—to take a less stressful job or even begin to plan for your retirement. In the past few decades, many American families have decided to "leave the fast lane behind." Some take less stressful jobs. Others open a small family business of their own. I've talked to people who down-sized their houses or moved to smaller towns. Less radical solutions include joining a fitness club or changing eating habits.

No matter what your score is, see your family doctor anyway. Annual wellness check-ups never hurt anybody.

First Aid for Stress

The following is a list of ten specific ways to manage and cope with the stress you face. These suggestions will not cure all of your stress-related problems, but they will certainly help you manage it in a more positive way. They can help prevent some of the serious problems that can occur if you are unable to cope with stress in your life. Think of these ideas as first aid for your stress.

1. **Monitor your stress patterns.** Begin keeping a journal. Recording stressful events and your responses to them is a good way to deal with

stress. Then go back to see if there are patterns in these situations that are more stressful for you than others. Change the things in your life that are possible to change.

2. **Work on your attitude.** In Chapter Seven: *How to Love Yourself,* we discussed ways to reprogram the negative messages you play in your head. Use a positive thoughts to lift yourself up. If you make a mistake, do what you can about it, forgive yourself and move on. Remind yourself that historically, all tough times have been temporary—for you and for everyone. At times, you may have to divert yourself from thinking negative thoughts. Try doing something for a person who needs your time and energy.

3. **Take responsibility for your own successes and failures.** You should learn as much from your mistakes as you do from your triumphs. Rethink the process that didn't quite work. Pat yourself on the back for accomplishments. Be patient with yourself as you learn, grow and change. Taking this attitude with yourself and other can have a major impact on reducing your stress.

4. **Balance your work and your personal life.** Your new task is to pay more attention to your personal life. Without a balanced life your stress level will always be too high. You are not your job. Take time out to be with your family and friends.

5. **Get support.** It is always easier when you don't have to face things alone. Even good things in your life are better when you can celebrate them with another. Talking with someone you trust, and who cares about you, alleviates a lot of stress and worry. You should never hesitate to seek help from all available sources of support, such as your employee assistance program, self-help groups, friends, religious organizations or professional counseling. The smartest thing you can ever do is to get help with your small problems before they become big ones.

6. **Examine what you think is expected of you.** Our society tells us we must be perfect, fast, strong and always say yes. In other words, we can't make mistakes or show weakness. We should always do what others ask and do it immediately. That's not realistic. As we've discussed, on the job our attitude should be: "I won't make unreasonable demands of you, if you don't make unreasonable demands of me." Try the same approach with yourself: treat yourself as you would want others to treat you. Know your limitations; accept them and set boundaries accordingly.

7. **Make large tasks more manageable.** When you have a large project to tackle, the stress of facing it can make it seem more difficult than it is. Break it down into smaller tasks, starting with the easiest parts first, so you feel

as if you're making headway. Take a break between tasks. Make sure you have realistic deadlines and ask for help when you need it. Don't forget the possibility that the person giving you the deadline doesn't know what is involved in terms of time and energy. Tell them. If at all possible, create a team and delegate tasks of the project to others. When you need more help with a specific task, set it aside while you go on to another task. Don't waste time waiting for help. Saving time and effort, anyway you can, will ease the stress of the project for you.

Here is a special note for those of you who tend to put off projects until the night or weekend before they are due. It's almost inevitable that there will be a glitch. Call it the "Fool's Rule." It might be that you can't get materials or resources you didn't know you would need to complete the project. Perhaps there will be a power failure that leaves your computer worthless. You may think the pressure to get it done will help motivate you, but that kind of stress would kill an elephant! Find a healthier way to complete projects, with time to spare.

8. Inject some humor into your work life. Take a little time to laugh. Laughter is good for you physically. It is one of the greatest emotional stress relievers known to humankind. In fact, humor is so successful as a stress reducer that it has spawned a whole new breed of consultants. John Cleese, of Monty Python and *A Fish Called Wanda* fame, uses humor therapy in his professional stress relief programs. Group laughter is one of the warmest sounds we know and it draws people in like a magnet. Shared humor helps people bond and build strong teams—as long as it is appropriate humor and not at anyone else's expense.

9. Take time for yourself. There are several ways to use time creatively to help reduce stress. If you have been working on a problem and can't seem to get anywhere with it, take a time-out and do something else. Work on something simpler, read a magazine, make a phone call or get a drink of water (not coffee or cola with caffeine). Getting your mind off the problem eases the stress of concentrating too hard on one thing. It allows you to relax a little and lets your thought processes refresh themselves. You can return to your task with a new perspective. Psychological studies show that creative ideas occur most easily when you let go of problems and indulge in something pleasurable. You should also allow yourself some off time once in a while. Take a mental break and let your mind wander. You might even accidentally wander into a new, creative idea. Planning regular quiet time to think things through and prioritize your goals is good for you. Learn what your concentration tolerance is during a workday. In other words, how long can you work continuously and still be productive? If you tend to taper off around 3:00 p.m. set your watch to beep and remind you when it's time to take a break. If possible, allow some time to unwind at lunch and when you get home from work. At night you should try to forget about work. Even if you bring work home, give yourself time to relax before doing it.

When you unwind, do something completely different from your job. Don't balance your checkbook or work on your taxes. Play a board game with your family members, watch a movie or go out to dinner. If you have a time-consuming commute home, don't get in your car, sitting in traffic with nothing to stew about but your work. Listen to an audio book or music that involves you. Form a carpool with some fun people. Take turns driving and talk about anything but your job. Before you know it, you'll be home.

If you don't have children on athletic teams who play their games in the early evening, find a team that needs more fans in their bleachers. Your local high school probably has an athletic competition every week that would welcome new "boosters." Get out there and yell and cheer and clap for someone else's kids. You will be amazed at how good you feel. You can even treat your family to an outing for a "drive-through" dessert.

Make a family rule that when a member comes through the door, after work or school, there will be no negative discussion with them for thirty minutes. Use your free time to jump in the shower and sing your heart out and "wash the stress right out of your hair." Do whatever it takes. Just like a car cannot change gears without the clutch, release your stress instead of compounding it, like grinding gears in your head. Even the good stress of your workday needs to be unloaded.

10. Go with the flow. Resisting change only increases stress. When you go with the flow, you will still have stress, but coping with it will be much less difficult because your attitude won't be magnifying it. Learning to accept change may be the most important way to keep stress from getting out of control. It is inevitable that there will be alterations in your job, company or even in your career field. If you fear it, you will only add more stress to your already stressful life. Of course it is only natural for human beings to fear change and worry about the future. But if you learn to look for the possibilities instead of the problems, you will find that you don't have as much to fear as you thought you did.

Sharon was an administrative assistant for fifteen years. She continued to grow and develop in her job in an insurance office, learning more about the industry all the time. She felt secure in her position, performing her familiar du-ties. She became so knowledgeable about the company's clients and their needs her boss decided he wanted her to step into a different role. He wasn't sure what the position would be, but he knew Sharon's valuable knowledge could help the company identify and service new clients.

The idea was frightening to Sharon at first. Her boss was asking her to take on a new position that wasn't even defined! He could only tell her about a few of the ideas he had for using her expertise to expand the company's market. She became overwhelmed by stress, as she feared that an ill-defined job function would lead to her failure and loss of a secure career. She continued to protest the change for a while, but her boss insisted that he wanted her to take the step.

Gradually Sharon began to think about the possibilities for her new position. Her boss's confidence in her abilities encouraged her. Eventually Sharon created her own title of marketing specialist and used her boss's ideas as a foundation for designing a whole new marketing program for the company. She experienced a new excitement about her job and found that she was more in control of her career than she had ever been.

Keeping your mind open to new possibilities and your body in good physical condition are the most positive steps you can take toward reducing the effects of stress in your life. As one adage points out, "When life gives you lemons, make lemonade." That's a good way of saying that you can decide to turn disadvantages into advantages if you are willing to try.

CHAPTER NINE

HOW TO LOVE THE CRITICISM YOU HATE

Without a doubt, anger and criticism can be major contributors to hating your job. Criticism can chip away at confidence, leaving an almost over-whelming sense of defeat in its wake. Anger toward a co-worker, employer or situation can burn with a destructive intensity.

Supervisors who understand the powerful skill of using constructive criticism can base an impressive career on it, in almost any field. A team leader with the ability to use constructive criticism in a positive way becomes a mentor, much like an athletic coach. They know the skills required to win, and how to get results out of each of their workers by cheering them on. These enlightened managers know how to help employees reach their potential on each project. While the skill of using positive criticism well—and receiving it in kind—can be an exciting formula for success, it is up to the company culture to make that formula the business standard for achieving success. If the methodology is not fostered, the result can be failure on all levels of the company. It is the differ-ence between a nurturing work environment and a group of people working in fear, trying to get through each day without feeling awful about their work and themselves.

Terry, a systems analyst at a large Midwestern university, creates that sense of defeat in his co-workers. He points out with discouraging consistency things his co-workers—and even his boss—aren't doing right. His approach represents criticism at its worst—it is both insulting and embarrassing to his colleagues.

Victoria, an accountant at a small medical supplies firm, struggles almost daily with the anger she feels about her work environment. "The left hand never knows what the right hand is doing," is the way she characterizes the lack of structure at her firm. When she submits suggestions to improve the company to her employer, she generally receives no response—which only angers her more.

These are only two examples of the corrosive effect anger and criticism can have on a job. Although they are not in themselves bad, if they are not handled well they can have a negative impact on job performance and morale. Let's examine further these two common—but not always well-managed—facets of the job.

The Give and Take of Criticism

Many people respond negatively to the word criticism, instantly associating it with harsh comments, hurt feelings and angry responses. But criticism does not have to be destructive, regardless of whether you are on the giving or receiving end. Instead, criticism can serve as a useful tool for improving job performance, motivating others and creating a sense of resolution as solutions are reached.

Be conscious of the spirit in which criticism is given. Are you prone to giving negative criticism? Ask yourself if you have lost perspective and humor because you are so focused on what others are doing wrong. Remember that if you are too critical, you are blocking the creative process that accompanies any job. Being critical in a negative way inhibits good relationships, produces retaliatory criticism and bruises much-needed good will among co-workers.

A negative critic will find himself talking about a co-worker behind their back, which fosters distrust and anger once that co-worker finds out it is happening. And they will find out!

- Negative criticism attacks. It says, "Do you really think you're going to get anywhere doing work like this?"

- Negative criticism threatens. "You'd better get on the stick with your computer skills or there will be some repercussions."

- Negative criticism insults. "How much time did you spend on your presentation? It was awful."

- Negative criticism embarrasses. "Hey, guys, let's put Debbie's work on the bulletin board as an example of what *not* to do."

You get the picture. This is the sort of criticism demonstrated by Terry, the systems analyst at the beginning of this chapter. Negative criticism is a destructive force that can cause irreparable damage to self-esteem, job productivity and attitude. On the "Why You Hate Your Job" list, it ranks on top for a lot of employees. But criticism doesn't have to get bad rap. Indeed, there are ways to criticize productively.

Think of it as teaching. You have information that can help someone learn how to produce better work. When you share that information, you are serving as an instructor of sorts, offering instructions on how to make good work *great*. Instead of criticizing someone for an obviously rushed presentation, you might say, "You did a good job! Am I right in thinking I didn't give you as much time to present your excellent information as you would have liked? Let's get together and talk about how you can format the information so that next time you can discuss each point in more detail within the time period. You can also show me how you formulate your presentation so I can allot the time you need." You've just taught your co-worker, through criticism, how to improve on his or her job. If the person has poor self-esteem and your experience is that he or she doesn't hear criticism well—they only take the negative nuances in your statement—you have taken any possible negative criticism on yourself. There is nothing left for them to take but encouragement to do even better next time, and you've make them feel like an important part of your job.

Build self-esteem. Letting a co-worker know that her work is valuable is a true self-esteem builder. When you tell her she is doing a good job, she will most likely be far more receptive to hearing how she can do an even better job next time.

Criticism can mean caring. People *can* feel that you care when you criticize. By expressing your concern, you are saying, "I care that you succeed on your job. Let me share with you a way that can boost your success."

Timing can be everything. Don't pick a moment when a co-worker is already depressed about something to start a discussion that can fuel negativity or defensiveness. If a co-worker is receiving praise, never deflate their joy by sharing criticism at that moment. Always ensure that your comments are private. Choose a time that is neutral and calm.

Make sure the comments can be implemented. Be sure the recipient can do something about the situation for which you are offering criticism. If it is too late to do anything about it, he or she will only become frustrated. Asking them to change direction in a project, with the same deadline, will give you a worker with no confidence to finish. Always talk about what can be done the next time.

Be specific. Vague criticisms can create a chasm of anxiety and doubt. Don't leave the recipient guessing; give an example of where you think she may be falling short and what you think she can do to improve. "Your voice is soft and I'm not sure everyone could hear you. If I had your talent with photography, I might have taken pictures of the products you showcased and used them in the presentation."

Listen. How does the recipient of your criticism feel afterward? Ask. Then listen closely to determine if she understands what you have said. Work to avoid mis-communication at the first sign of trouble.

Avoid the "should." How are you coming across? Are the first words out of your mouth, "You know, you should really write your report this way"? When you remain open and instructive, instead of rigid and pedantic, your criticism is more likely to gain acceptance. Open up the menu of options and allow the person to think creatively. Given permission to think about it with enthusiasm, the person may come up with something even better.

Don't push. Pushing the person you're criticizing to take your suggested action puts stress on the recipient. It shows that you are far more concerned with seeing your ideas implemented than your co-worker's well-being.

When possible, consider temperaments. The command-person will not respond to criticism in the same way the support-person will. Keep in mind that a sensitive co-worker could require a more delicate approach, whereas the matter-of-fact detail-person colleague will value a tactful, yet more direct, discussion.

Talk about rewards. Tell the person you are criticizing how he will benefit from taking a certain action. Unless the person lives to please you, they won't care if something will make you happy just because they do it your way. Remind them of the powerful payoffs to their career which could come from responding positively to criticism.

Your Response

Now that you know how to give criticism, and how powerful it can be, how do you take it? Take a brief look at something you do that could cause someone to criticize you. Maybe you make mistakes. Mess-ups, miscalculations, failed ideas and just plain "I blew its!" are bound to happen. But, like anger, it's the way you respond to the mistakes that makes the difference.

First of all, it is important to remember to take responsibility for your failures as well as your successes. Look at the mistakes and failures as necessary and valuable life lessons. Don't let your response to them (and the resultant criticism) sabotage the rest of your work life.

Realize that successful people actually make more mistakes than unsuccessful people do. What that means is they keep trying far longer than unsuccessful people who quit or give up after a few failures. They know that a spectacular success will justify all the failures along the way. How many tries do you think it took Thomas Edison to get the light bulb or the phonograph to work right?

Don't let mistakes weigh you down. You may go through periods where you make more mistakes than at other times: the greater the stress of the situation, the greater the chance of making mistakes. Remember to be patient with yourself, learn from the difficulties and move on.

Here comes the boss or a co-worker anxious to share a few "suggestions" about what you did and how it could be handled better in the future! How do you take criticism?

Be willing to learn. You can take an active stance. Ask others how you can improve. Be open to what they say. If you realize that criticism is a way to help you measure your performance and improve upon it, you'll welcome it.

Listen and learn. Even if you have not sought the correction, turn off the tendency to respond defensively. Truly listen to the criticism. If it is productive, try to respond positively in return.

Don't put yourself down. Be kind to yourself. Don't decide that you have totally botched the project because someone has pointed out a way it could be improved for future presentations. You are not a total failure at work because one suggestion has been made on how you can work more effectively in the future.

Ask for more. Once you are comfortable with receiving criticism, express gratitude for the help. Ask for more suggestions.

Anger: The Misunderstood Emotion

Anger is one of the most common emotions human beings face, especially in the work world. But it is also one of the most misunderstood. Sometimes, it is inappropriately dealt with at work or ignored altogether.

First realize feeling anger is OK. You may be hearing some of those old programming tapes from your childhood that told you anger was bad. If you were punished or ignored for expressing anger, you probably have a difficult time dealing with it now. But, there is nothing wrong with *feeling* anger. It is an emotion like any other and is not wrong in itself. There are good reasons for feeling anger: injustice, a setback or a tragedy are all possible reasons. The problem can be your response.

You can probably think of an instance where it is not all right to express your anger. Most of us tend to want to repress it. Depending on our temperament, the more vocal command-persons and people-persons will more readily express anger, but even they can be controlled by childhood programming.

Can you think of an instance when you feel OK about expressing anger? If you answered no, consider this: Do you ever have a problem controlling your expression of anger? If you said yes, you probably know that this is a double whammy. You believe it's wrong to get angry, yet you have a hard time not getting angry! How does that add up? You'll have major stress. The best way to avoid being upset by this emotion is to decide that it is OK to feel anger. But when is it all right to express it, and how should it be expressed?

There are basically two ways to express anger: outwardly and inwardly. The outward expression may be manifested in rage or "explosions." The inward expression may show up as resentment and bitterness. The outward expression demonstrates itself directly to the object of the anger, such as yelling at a person or kicking a desk. The inward expression cannot be shown directly to the object of the anger, for whatever reason, so it turns in on the angry person. Both of these responses create an unhealthy state of mind and can result in stress-related illnesses such as heart disease and ulcers.

You need to feel your anger, but neither of the above responses is the best way to express it. There is a constructive way to use anger as a motivating force, and it can be outward or inward. If a co-worker has done something that you specifically asked him not to do—say he has destroyed a project you were both working on—you have a right to be angry. But it won't help either of you if you go to him and fly into a rage, provoking his defensive anger as well. Neither will it resolve the situation if you don't say anything and keep your anger inside. Usually, repressed anger builds into full-fledged resentment that damages your ability to work with others.

Here's how to deal with the co-worker who messed up your project: You need to confront the person and let him or her know you are angry. You asked him to perform the task a certain way for a reason, and the fact the project is now in ruins proves your point. He should learn from the mistake he has made and you are the person who can teach him. Open confrontation is a valid approach, provided you are not patronizing. Remember, someday the shoe could be on the other foot, and that person may be confronting you.

Your anger could propel you to say something ill-considered to your errant co-worker. Instead, try to say something constructive. Let your anger inspire you to say to yourself, "Yes, I have a valid reason to correct this person." Approach him when you are calm, controlled and rational. Explain the error, the consequences and the solution. Further, explain how you can work together to straighten out the problem. You can help dissipate the tension by remaining calm and in control. This approach practically guarantees good results. You will be able to maintain a good relationship with the co-worker and probably salvage the project too. Both of you will feel better about the incident, and it could even strengthen your working relationship.

Let's turn the tables around. Suppose you are on the receiving end of someone's anger. What is the best way to respond? If a colleague or boss is screaming at you, you will not help anything by screaming back—even if you feel justified. First, you need to show that you accept the other person's feelings and are willing to *try to understand* what he or she is communicating with you. In other words, "Yes, I see that you are angry. I'm willing to find out what I've done to warrant your anger and try to fix it if I can." Admit your fault or part in the problem, if it is valid. Offer your sincere apology and willingness to make amends.

If you are not responsible, don't become defensive. Try to explain as rationally as you can your role in the situation. Try to convey that, though you were not to blame for the person's anger, you do acknowledge their emotion and are willing to help in anyway you can. Sometimes, people just need a sign their anger—even at themselves—is understood by another person. Low-key nonverbal responses also help diffuse anger. People tend to see and hear things in an exaggerated way when they are angry, so a quiet tone of voice and relaxed but attentive posture can have a calming effect. Maintain steady eye contact while he vents his anger and try not to interrupt. Letting him get it off his chest shows respect for his feelings and a willingness to cooperate to solve the problem. Listening to the other person, taking his feelings seriously, and remaining calm under pressure are all keys to successful communication.

Of course, if a person becomes violent or abusive, you should calmly tell him or her that you are willing to work out the problem. Explain that you don't think it's a good time to continue the discussion, then quietly leave. There is little more you can do in a situation like this.

Deflecting someone else's anger. How do you deal with anger that another person is holding in? If you feel that someone is angry with you, but he or she seems unwilling to be direct, there are three ways to respond.

If the reasons for the outburst are unclear to you, first examine what he is *not* saying. Many people lash out and it is hard to understand what the problem is. Try to determine the possible causes for his anger. If you can find out the cause and simply change something you are doing, you may be able to resolve the problem without confrontation. This is risky, however, because your solution may not be accurate—and it depends on a bit of mind reading.

Second, you can choose to ignore the negative messages being sent by a co-worker. If he really has a problem, he can just come out and tell you. This is also risky because it does nothing to resolve the issue, which may only grow worse.

The third possible response is the most appropriate. You may need a confrontation. Although unpleasant, it is far more productive than letting a misunderstanding continue unchecked. Tension manages to spill over to others until there are more uncomfortable co-workers than just the two of you. Perhaps the other person just doesn't have the skill to approach another when the issue is anger—even when the anger turns out to be valid. Help him or her! Show them the way. Let them know that it is safe to express anger by taking the initiative and telling him you feel something is wrong. Show that you are willing to work things out if you have done something to offend him. Most of the time, people appreciate a sincere effort to work out issues that can be resolved together. If that doesn't work and he is still angry, at least you've done your part. You can't force the other person to come forward.

There are practical ways to deal with anger. Let's go back to Victoria, the angry accountant mentioned earlier, to see how she can apply these principles to the anger she experiences on the job.

Let go of petty annoyances. Victoria has some valid problems with the way the company is operating. However, things have reached the point where every small irritation sets her teeth on edge. Although she certainly should express her concerns about what she sees as major flaws in the firm's operations, she is only feeding the flames of destructive anger by holding on to the smallest incident. By letting go of petty annoyances, she can focus constructively on the issues that should be addressed with her employer. Not only that, Victoria will also experience less stress if she is not on the lookout for one more minor incident to add to her stockpile of resentments.

Don't feed on the anger of others. Victoria is not alone in her feelings of frustration and anger with her company. Several of her co-workers share those feelings, and her office is often the setting for discussions that center almost exclusively on what the company is doing wrong and how difficult it is to work there. Granted, it's only natural to want to let off some steam on occasion, but constant negative discussions accomplish nothing except to fuel the flames of discontent and hopelessness about the job situation.

Victoria would be better off directing her conversations with her co-workers to possible solutions. If those resolutions have been ignored, as they have been in Victoria's case, then she and her co-workers should address the problem. Creating an environment of positive influence with co-workers to bring about change is far more effective than running together in a vicious circle of fault-finding and complaining.

Watch what you say out of anger. Victoria has occasionally been careless about vocalizing her anger with the company and more than once has made comments that are inappropriate in her office setting. This could not only damage her growth in the company; it could hurt her credibility when she does present her concerns to management. There is something to be said for the adage "bite the bullet—especially if it means you will keep from shooting yourself in the foot." Carefully choosing your words, even in the face of circumstances that cause justifiable anger, leaves your dignity and integrity intact.

Honest communication is the key. One of Victoria's sources of anger comes from the fact that she has approached the company's management about her concerns and the response has been unsatisfactory. If you have been in the same situation, you know how frustrating it is when you feel ignored.

So what do you do? In Victoria's case, she can call a halt to the anger that's building inside and open an honest dialogue with her management. She might say: "I'm concerned that perhaps we're not communicating clearly with each other. Can we sit down and further discuss the topics I've brought to your attention?" By confronting management in a way that is not defensive or negative, she would demonstrate persistence and subtly call for management to take part in an exchange. Keeping the door of communication open will keep anger from building when other doors are closed.

Attitude and Anger. Your attitude is the most important element in handling anger. It controls your response to it and plays an important role in affecting other people's reactions to you.

Remember three things about anger:

1. It is okay to feel angry—it is your response that counts.

2. Don't make important decisions while you're angry, as your ability to think rationally is impaired.

3. Don't make judgments about people while either you or they are angry. Instead, concentrating on how you can change yourself and your own responses will make anger a lot easier to handle.

Dealing with On-the-Job Abuse

In today's workplace, thousands of people fall victim to verbal and emotional abuse. Don't perpetuate it with silence. Never be afraid to report abuse. One reason people continue verbal, emotional and physical mistreatment of others is that no one stops them. You don't have to confront this person directly—in fact it's unwise to do so. Report it to your boss. The abuse becomes the responsibility of the employer when a co-worker feels victimized by it. If it is not reported, and continues unabated, it may even escalate to physical violence or threats of such.

If the abuser is the boss, your employment situation is untenable. If you can't leave the job, try telling your boss that you just can't work in an environment of fear. Once you've brought your feelings to his or her attention, they may be surprised that the temper tantrums are taken as abuse. If you present it as your problem—that you cannot produce quality work when you feel threatened—you may find that the behavior stops.

Recently, I found myself in a situation where I felt violated by a verbal exchange. I was so shocked by the language used that I had a delayed reaction. Three days after the event, I wrote a letter to the president of the organization and sent copies to the gentlemen who used the language. In the letter, I described the nature of our business meeting, how I felt about their choice of words, my need for the elimination of such language in future meetings and the consequences of any repeated exchange. It never happened again.

Anger and *criticism*—those two words with negative connotations—can be handled in a way that produces good results on your job. Learning to manage them can greatly relive your hatred of your job. But the solution isn't always permanent. You may have to return to this chapter for a healthy reminder that out of confrontations can come tremendous growth.

CHAPTER TEN
LEAVING THE JOB YOU HATE

Wouldn't it be great if we all graduated from high school knowing our strengths and talents, clear on what particular field of employment was best for us? Wouldn't it be even better if we were all accepted to attend—on full scholarship (as long as we are dreaming)—the university that offers the best instructors in that field? We would be their favorite students, and they would ask to be our mentors. They would make sure that the most progressive company hired us. We would start with a generous starting salary and incredible benefits. Our job would be located in a great community where we were surrounded by family and friends. The economy would always be growing and our jobs would never be downsized.

But it's just not that way, is it? Few are really sure what they are "supposed" to be doing. People try to chart a career path, hoping that each job will help their employment future. Sometimes they must compromise and take a job that is not a first choice, but is still on the road to a goal. Many other times, workers take employment that may not be quite right for them because they are driven by economic factors or family pressures—childcare, chronic illness of a family member, aging parent care. However, that doesn't mean one has to be stuck in an unfulfilling job for the rest of time.

In Chapter One, we met several workers who were so dissatisfied with their jobs they toyed with the idea of quitting. They felt that a change in their relationship with their company robbed them of their love for their job. In every instance, their employers had no idea they were close to losing a valued employee. No worker should wait until their situations have become so stressful that they would consider quitting before making a plan or giving their employer the opportunity in supporting the burden they carry.

This chapter is designed to help you make one last effort to salvage your job before you walk out. But if you must leave, there are ways to do it. Making sure your reasons are clearly defined is important, too.

Take a weekend or a day off when you don't have anything major occupying your thoughts to think objectively about your job. Analyze the direction you are taking in your life. You might take a look at your current résumé (if you don't have one, write one now) and think about your previous employment. Compare those to the job you have now. Has your work history followed a pattern? Have you reached your goal, or are you moving away from it? Do you need to set a new or a more realistic objective in light of changes in your personal life?

Even if you've been in the same occupation for twenty years, you may decide you want to take a risk and change careers. Perhaps upon further reflection you will conclude that staying with what you are doing now is not only the most practical decision, but the most rewarding. There is no right or wrong choice. It all depends on what is most fulfilling for you and pays the bills.

Analyze Your Current Job

Draw a line down the middle of a sheet of paper. Write your personal strengths on one side and your personal weaknesses on the other. Now divide another sheet of paper down the middle. On the first sheet, write your personal strengths on the left side and your weaknesses on the right. They don't have to be in any particular order; just write them down as you think of them. On the next sheet, put down what you like doing in your current job on the left side and what you don't on the right.

Here is a sample list that was done by one of my seminar participants who was an advertising copywriter.

Personal Strengths	Personal Weaknesses
Good writer	Not a good speaker
Organized	Uncomfortable as a leader
Detail-oriented	Sometimes overly detailed
Precise, accurate	Sometimes over critical
Can analyze facts, data	Not socially outgoing

Good listener	Don't like pressure
Good observer	Need supportive leadership
Work independently	Sometimes get set in my ways
Enjoy teamwork	Don't like committee work
Enjoy planning	Don't like to push people
Enjoy research	Need some structure from management
Enjoy learning new things	Don't handle personal criticism well
Continually study my field	Don't like managing budgets

Job Likes	Job Dislikes
Writing ads	Getting quotes on jobs
Writing marketing plans	Having to deal with vendors
Planning strategies	Having to do others' work
Researching clients' business	Dealing with rude or gruff people
Analyzing client's needs	Constant pressure to produce
Using research creatively	Having my research misquoted
Freedom to be creative	Presenting to a group
Freedom to work independently	Unrealistic expectations of boss
Working in creative teams	Substituting for receptionist
Analyzing market data	Not being given enough time

Now compare these two lists. You'll most likely find that your strengths correspond to what you like to do. Your weaknesses correspond to what you don't. It is normal to like what you do well and dislike what you don't. What you like and dislike have a lot to do with your personality type. People-persons love dealing with people and hate doing paperwork. Detail-persons, on the other hand, enjoy the reverse. A support-person may be unhappy in a position where he or she must take charge and make quick decisions, but the command-person loves that kind of challenge. The command-person is bored and frustrated with a position that is structured and predictable.

Analyze your lists carefully. Once you have done this simple exercise, you may realize the reasons for liking or disliking your job. Every job will have some aspects you don't like, but if your lists are out of balance, if you are doing a lot of things you don't like to do or are not good at, you may be in the wrong job. If you are doing what you are good at, but you hate a lot of the things you have to do, your job may have changed from what it was when you first started. Perhaps you like what you are doing, but problems frustrate you, keeping you from doing your job the way you feel you could.

Once you have studied your lists and determined where your problem areas are, you may want to talk to your boss about how you feel. If you approach your boss with the attitude that you want to do a better job you should get a favorable response. Most employers appreciate an employee's willingness to improve his or her performance. Resolving the things that you hate about your job will enrich your work.

Evaluating Your Options

Maybe, instead of being helpful and listening to your concerns about your job, your boss says, "Find another job!" Perhaps there is no way to make your job better. When you are thinking about quitting, the main thing you need to ask yourself is, "Am I in a no-win situation?" If the answer is yes, it is time to move on. Here are a few examples of situations that may provoke a job change.

Your job duties have changed radically from when you were hired. Perhaps due to reorganization and cutbacks in your company, your position has changed so much that you are no longer doing what you were originally hired to do.

Lucinda was a marketing manager in a large regional bank. She handled all the marketing and advertising projects for her branch. She loved the creativity and responsibility of the position. There was no question that she was good at her job, but due to mergers and subsequent downsizing, the regional headquarters in another city began to handle all of these responsibilities. Lucinda was given more market research work, which was not as creative and interesting as her previous duties. She liked her work less, since she was not performing the work she really did well. She began to think about exploring other opportunities, but she hesitated because she was receiving excellent pay and benefits and liked her co-workers.

Lucinda realized that monetary compensation is not always the most important part of a job. She realized that her strengths were not being fully utilized and chances were that they never would be again in that position. Lucinda was perfectly justified in leaving that job, and she did it the *smart* way. She began discretely talking to people she knew in other companies, seeking out interviews even if there were no current job openings. That way she was able to discuss possible job changes and test the waters to see what was out there. She made sure to say that the dissatisfaction was with her own career direction. She did not speak against the company, her supervisors or her co-workers. When a position became available in one of the companies she had talked with, Lucinda was their top choice.

Your career field has changed and you are no longer able to adapt. Due to the technological revolution, many career fields are radically changing. Numerous fields have become almost fully computerized, even the commercial art field. Where graphic designers and illustrators once relied on their drawing skills, they are now required almost universally to do everything on computer. Artists who had been in the business for twenty or thirty years began to lose their jobs to younger workers whose art skills are totally computer-dependent.

Some artists adapted well to the new computer systems, but it was painful for artists such as Ellen and Jack, who worked in an advertising department for more than twenty years, to have young computer artists who couldn't even draw by hand, favored over them. Being close to retirement age, Jack chose to take early retirement rather than learn a whole new system at his age. Ellen chose to resign and open her own small business selling prints of her paintings by catalog. Both made choices to quit their jobs and pursue other options that made them happier, even though their financial rewards may not have been as great.

If you have been in a career field for many years and find that it is changing more than you feel comfortable adapting to, it may be time to consider other options. Your best bet is to study other related fields and find out how you can adapt your current skills and experience to them.

Your company or entire industry may be unstable. Always keep up with the economic and competitive trends in your industry, as well as with the technological changes. Read trade and business journals that monitor these changes. Consider how this impacts your job—is your position threatened? Make a list of things you can do to prepare if you need to leave. You will have a plan to fall back on if things begin to look bleak.

The political winds have changed and you no longer fit in. Sometimes new management of a company can change the political atmosphere so much with that your work style and philosophy are no longer accepted. You may see evidence of in the loss of certain responsibilities or privileges. You may be passed over for raises and promotions, have difficulty getting feedback from superiors or find your ideas and projects ignored. If that continues for more than a few weeks and your boss is reluctant to discuss your future with the company, it is usually a sign that there is definite trouble looming. You may have done nothing wrong, but the political winds have obviously shifted against you. It is a good time to start exploring your options outside the company.

The organization's values are no longer acceptable. Often with a political change, there is also a change in company values. Getting a job done quickly may suddenly take precedence over getting it done right. Procedures may change to the point that they are questionable or even unethical. You might try adapting your values to the new ones, but if they are basically unacceptable to you, you will not be happy doing this. You might also try to effect a change in values or return to previous ones, but don't push so hard that you damage your own image with the company. If you choose to remain and fight, you will almost certainly be branded as an employee who refuses to be a team player. You don't need to be in an even more stressful situation. If you've tried going through channels, talking with your boss and being patient all to no avail, you probably should try to get out before your career, your self-esteem or your health suffers.

Reasons to Quit a Job: the New Employer's Point of View

From your future boss' point of view, a person who leaves a good job is a bit suspect. Prospective employers must think like people buying a used car—nobody wants to take on someone else's problems. The following reasons are considered valid reasons to leave a job:

- An offer from another company with better chances for advancement toward your goal

- An offer from another company with better job security

- An offer from another company with much better salary and benefits package

- An offer to work with a known mentor in your field or another opportunity that furthers or updates your skills in your career field

- Starting your own business without taking clients or business knowledge away from your former employer.

- Leaving a boss or business culture that is known to be difficult or unethical. This is can be very tricky as one must explain the situation without being negative, while still portraying the difficulty.

- Moving more than fifty miles to a better area for your family or to secure necessary medical care for a family member

Reasons for quitting a job must be true, honest and verifiable. When interviewing for a new job, you will walk a thin line; discuss the positive about your current company and be very discrete about the negative. No new employer likes disloyalty in an employee—even if it is toward a competitor. And neither should you. If an interviewer seems to encourage your disloyalty, you have to wonder if you want to work for him or her.

Show that you have thought long and hard about your decision, that you have made a plan to make the decision work and that you will be a good addition to the new company. If you left to move to a job that offered better chances to reach your career goals, highlight those goals on your résumé and how the job change worked in favor of reaching your goals.

Reasons that make employers hesitant about hiring you include:

- List of on-going personal problems, such as a messy divorce, wanting to avoid paying child support, avoidable financial problems or court-ordered employer garnishments.

- Blaming the boss or co-workers for past job performance. Stating that one could not get along with, or plain not liking, the boss or co-workers.

- Stating that you left because of too much work for too little pay—many companies have the same constraints.

- Your résumé shows way too many jobs in a short period of time—say three jobs in a year. Also periods without any verifiable employment at all.

- Unethical work—you were working "off-the-books" for cash or you allowed others to use your credentials or license for work that you did not do. No boss wants someone who suddenly wants to "come-clean" on his or her dime.

If you left a job for one of these five reasons, rethink how it will show on your résumé. For example, if you left because of poor personal choices, show that you have since taken control of your life; cleaned up your credit, paid your child support or settled into a stable personal life. It may be a good idea to carry new Court Orders for a reduced alimony or other obligation to prove you have things under control. Many companies do credit checks now, so these things may come up even if you haven't disclosed your problems. Show that you learned from your mistakes, instead of running from them with no interest in improving the situation.

(Reset)

How Not to Quit Your Job

If you decide to quit a job, always keep your eye on a positive and clean exit, no matter how you feel or your reasons for leaving. Unfortunately, this will be the hardest possible time to remain calm and upbeat—but you absolutely must. What you do at work as you leave the company is as important as your entire tenure. What follows are a few "don'ts" that could sabotage your job change.

<u>Don't</u> **burn your bridges.** You might feel like telling off the boss who made you miserable or quitting without notice, but that could hurt you down the road. You may need this company or its people someday, not only as references, but as potentially valuable contacts. You don't think it's possible? Think again. Your new employer could get bought out by the same company you are leaving and—surprise!—you are working for the same people again. Many large government contracts are awarded to more than one company, and they may be asked to work together. Perhaps your old company will simply become a customer of your new one. You don't want to be responsible for your new employer losing business, do you? The old "gets along well with others" trait from grade school will serve you well, whether you are working in a different company or if you decide to go into business yourself.

<u>Don't</u> **use your letter of resignation to let the top management know "what's really going on around here."** It's likely they won't understand your point and your reputation will be ruined. The same goes for an Exit Interview if your company uses that tool. Nothing negative you say will be recorded—and you could ruin the good standing you worked for years to get and keep. It's just not worth it. There is nothing to gain by being negative.

<u>Don't</u> **let your work slump or broadcast your bad feelings while you are looking for another job.** Be discrete about your job search. Continue to produce a high level of quality work. If you don't, you could damage your reference from this company and your image with other companies that contact this one. Doing a poor job and bad-mouthing your employer can also get you fired! That won't look good on your résumé and you will never be able to change it.

<u>Don't</u> **feel guilty.** This is most important. You are acting in your best self-interest. Your company would not hesitate to act in its own best interest in order to survive. As long as you have given them your best work, you don't owe them anything else. This is especially true if the company has not fully used your abilities.

Don't endanger yourself financially. It is never advisable to leave your current job without a solid new job lined up unless you absolutely have to. Don't risk your hard-won seniority with a current company to start at the bottom with a new one without a very good reason. If you don't have a job lined up when you quit, make sure you have savings that will support your regular expenses for at least six months. It normally takes about that amount of time to find an equivalent employment position, but in a sluggish economy it could take much longer.

How to Leave Your Job Positively

Write a letter of resignation expressing gratitude for the time you were with the company. It may be hard, but try to think of *something* for which you are thankful. Remember that it is likely you gained new skills. Show your appreciation for that opportunity to learn. In your letter, emphasize that your decision to leave is based on personal career needs.

Give at least two weeks' notice, offering to complete as much work as possible in that time.

Prepare a small packet with a schedule of anticipated work for the next person in your job.

List the resources needed for your position—where to get them and how to get help for projects.

If you are comfortable, **leave your home telephone number in your desk** with a note to your replacement to call you at home if they are desperate for information only you would have, like a filing system that made sense to you and you alone. Anticipating the needs of the person who will be hired to replace you is the right thing to do and sets a positive tone. It shows you to be a class act to your co-workers and the person who replaces you. That kind of office-talk gets around.

Leaving your Job to Start Your Own Business

Leaving your job to start your own business can be a good reason to leave your current job. Careful planning will give your dream of becoming an entrepreneur the best chance and make you look more professional to others. As you prepare, consider these important questions:

Do you have enough money to start a business? Plan for at least one year of taking no income from your new business. You will probably need to plow any profits back into it. Contact the Small Business Administration in your area or speak to a business banker.

Do you have a clear business plan? How will you produce your goods, distribute them, advertise and service your clients? Know before you start.

Can you take the pressure and responsibility of others depending on you? Not everyone is cut out to be the prime decision maker, as we discussed in Chapter Three: *How to Love the Personality You Hate.* Public records show that the road to local Bankruptcy Courts is paved with great employees who became failed business owners.

- Have you properly researched all the legal licenses and permits necessary for your business in your local area? Investigate the requirements carefully. Consult a business attorney and business insurance agent.

- What is the real motive for creating this company? Never quit and start your own business just to "get back" at your employer.

- Are you planning to take your former employer's customers or your former co-workers to start your business? That is unethical and immediately sets you up with an unpleasant reputation. Plan a business model that serves different customers than your old employer. You never know who your future clientele may be. It could be your old company!

These questions are just to get you thinking about whether you should start your own company. If you feel this is the right step for you, do lots of research. There are many excellent books on the subject of starting a business, and more about starting up a company in your particular field of endeavor.

The Option for Kenny

You will recall Kenny from Chapter One and his dilemma of declining job satisfaction due to the amount of travel he did, even though he was well compensated by his employer. He attended a seminar I conducted for his company on how best to utilize the capabilities of every employee. Just as with many other seminar attendees, I hoped to give Kenny the tools to continue with this company, and to inspire his employers to show him how valuable he was.

I did a follow-up one-on-one session with him, as I do with all seminar participants who request it. Kenny was a great participant in that he wrote out a plan, using the information from my speech, to figure out a way to continue in the job he loved so much. The stress of travel, leaving his wife and son for such long stretches, and being available to his clients all the time, was threatening his health. His eating habits, fast food on the run—usually in airports—were taking their toll. His wife had hinted that he would have to choose between his job and his family. Kenny told me that he promised his wife that his personal life would come first and his job second. His son hardly knew him, and he was very unhappy about this particular development. He desperately wanted to find a way to make it all work out. He told me he was willing to take a pay cut, if only he could make his family feel more important by spending more time at home.

Kenny was approached by his company's competitors and the offers were great. One offered him the opportunity to move him anywhere his family wanted to live; close to family or friends who could provide his wife with a nurturing community. When this company approached him for the second time, they suggested another job that included an assistant to cut down on his travel time. A different company asked him if he would be interested in a position as an instructor, where he would stay in his own office. Although Kenny felt too much loyalty for the company that virtually created his career to consider seriously other employment offers, he was excited about how creative other personnel offices could be in providing a more healthy and supportive work environment.

Kenny put his suggestions—compiled from our sessions together and the outside offers he was getting—to his boss. He wanted to stay and work out the problems. Unfortunately, the company—whether it was justified to them by the corporate culture, the office politics, the management had become hidebound—could not, or would not change. They could not picture different job positions, new company flow charts, rewritten job descriptions or benefits that would actually be beneficial to a mature employee with a family who depended on them.

From my seminar, I knew Kenny wasn't the only employee who had changed since being hired and needed a job re-evaluation. The stress level was too high in many of the other employees, but like Kenny, they continued to really love what they did for a living. They felt lucky to have been hired by this company. Eventually, they will have to decide whether they will continue being stressed by their job or move on. And this company will apparently never understand why they cannot retain good people.

Kenny was sad to leave, but felt his choice was clear. His letter of resignation said he had an offer that would enhance his life, rather than just his career.

He went with the company that offered to move his family back to their home vicinity. His wife and son were delighted that they would be seeing much more of him. Kenny had never quit a job before, but it was a decision he had to make.

CHAPTER ELEVEN
LOSING THE JOB YOU LOVE

Whitney, a project coordinator for an event-planning firm, never saw it coming. She was called into her supervisor's office and fifteen minutes later she was walking down the hall to her cubicle to pack up her things. She was suddenly without a job. Stunned and dazed, she managed to box her personal items and leave the building, wondering through the haze of confusion about what she would do now.

In Whitney's case, her company was at fault. It wasn't able to sustain the number of its employees because it had grown too quickly and, because of bad management, was teetering on the brink of financial disaster. The easy solution was to let some of its employees go.

If you are like Whitney—a self-described "workaholic"—the loss of a job is like having a part of yourself cut off. She had an attachment to her work that sometimes excluded family and friends. This was a plus for her employer, who got twice the amount of work out of her. However, it only served to make her more isolated when she lost the employment to which she had dedicated her life.

Whitney began to feel dislocated and alone after several weeks of fruitless job searching. Her self-esteem suffered, her desire to continue looking for a job dwindled with each rejection letter and her mounting frustration was turning to bitterness.

What can you do when you lose the job you love? How can you cope? What follows are some methods to help you deal with the painful separation from a job that had become the driving force in your life.

Coping Strategies

Allow Yourself to Grieve

Mourn the job that was so important to you. As with any loss, it is only natural to want to give in to the pain of separation. Many studies over the years have shown that job loss is high on the list of traumatic life experiences. Allow yourself to experience the tears, the anger and the grief over losing your job. Otherwise, you will find yourself denying the pain of the event. Denial creates a web of self-deception that can eventually trap you into destructive depression and rage.

Although there is no set time frame for the grieving period, it is important to note that if you find yourself experiencing a lasting feeling of helplessness and hopelessness, your grief has deepened. If it becomes depression, you should seek medical help or professional counseling immediately. The purpose of grieving is to purge and eventually put the strong initial emotions behind you. If, instead, your grief grows, get professional help and stick with it until you feel more positive. Your new-found confidence will improve your chances with new job interviews.

Put the Job in Perspective

If you are like Whitney, you don't know where the job begins and you end. You and your job have become one. Your identity has become so deeply entwined with the job that you feel anonymous without it. There is a lack of balance and perspective in your life.

While joblessness is very uncomfortable, it can be a positive turning point. Now you can ask yourself, *Have I been consumed with this job to the exclusion of family, personal friends, spiritual, physical or emotional growth? Have I stopped taking care of myself with nutritional meals and regular medical and dental appointments?* Often, a deep attachment to a job reflects a struggle with self-esteem—the job compensates for what you perceive as a lack of ability or strength in other areas of your life. As you review Chapter Seven: *How to Love Yourself,* you may want to pursue a more personal growth process by talking with your pastor or counselor and spending time in prayer or meditation.

It is important to feel fulfilled in your job. But when the job replaces other components necessary to a healthy lifestyle, it is time to get a new perspective.

Confront Your Role in the Job Loss

Now is not the time to beat yourself up. This is a vulnerable time for you, so be gentle with yourself. Don't berate yourself about the things that can stand improvement. Just because you are examining your job performance doesn't mean you should place yourself under a microscope of criticism. Remind yourself of the things you do well—your dedication, accomplishments, successes and so on.

Most likely your company let you go because, like Whitney's situation, they made some mistakes that you are paying for. However, if you think your job performance played a part in your dismissal, look at it squarely and determine how you can best improve the next time around. If any self-evaluation is called for, do it as soon as you are comfortable with the idea.

This is a great time to dust off your résumé and take a good look at the reasons you left other jobs. If you were fired for cause from your last job, work to strengthen your references. Ask your former co-workers, at the highest levels possible, to write letters of recommendation for you. Think about what references you might get from previous employers.

If you can identify areas that need improvements, take a class or find someone who is objective and willing to be your job coach. Anything you can do to make a negative action result in a more positive employee is just what that new employer is looking for. Make it happen now. In your cover letter you can say something like, "I was not a strong enough team builder to be a supervisor at that time. I have since studied an area that I can specialize in, with little or no supervision, and have more to offer my co-workers in my next job." A true statement like that can turn any poor reference around.

Find a Reason to Get up Every Day

Like Whitney, you may be feeling discouraged over the length of time it's taking to get a new job. But you should not give in to the inertia that can plague a prolonged job search. In order to beat the desire to pull the covers over your head and stay in bed, decide to set and meet at least one goal for yourself every day. The goal should involve your job search: making phone calls, sending out résumés, reading the want ads, networking and so on. But if it takes deciding that you just want to see a movie, or take your shaggy dog to the vet, by all means, let that goal get you started.

The idea is to keep moving—not to the point of exhaustion—but to maintain the habit of daily activity that you developed when you were working. Your activities may have changed, but you can still be productive. The end result can eventually be a new job that you love.

Join a Support Group

If you don't have a group of unemployed persons in your community who meet to talk about their experiences, form one! Unfortunately, there are few places in the country where folks haven't been forced to tighten their personal belts. So there are probably many people who would respond to an ad in the paper about forming such a group.

Support groups are not meant to create a "misery loves company" situation. The best groups provide encouragement, education and feedback to one another as they face a shared difficult situation together. You can create friendships, take your mind off yourself by concentrating on the needs of others, and even discover new opportunities in employment that you may not have considered.

There are many support services being offered by the government for those who are jobless. This is not Welfare, but different services available for various jobs. If you need tools or reference books, for example, it is possible that you can be provided with them. These support services are designed to get you back to work—at no or low-cost. Make some calls and find out what might be available for you.

Keep the Lines of Communication Open

Spouses, children, friends and family members are those who are most concerned about your well-being; but they may be the very ones you avoid talking to. Don't hide your feelings. If you don't share your concerns, you will feel even more stressed. Let people know how things are going, what you are hoping for and how they can help. Borrow an outfit from a friend for a job interview. Others want to help; they just don't know what to do. Ask someone in your field to spend a few hours bouncing ideas around. Many people get just the job they want when people they know have valuable information. Neighbors, friends and fellow church members all know other people. Companies that are looking to hire usually put the word out. If you can get an interview before twenty people respond to a want ad, you may save the company the money it takes to advertise for a new employee.

More Coping Strategies

Don't expect too much from yourself. Although it is important to set daily goals for yourself, try not to overdo it. If you are a classic workaholic, you will put as much drive into your job search as you did into your job. But don't go into overload. Balance your day with activities that don't require a lot of mental energy, which will help to minimize stress.

Exercise. This may seem like more effort than you are prepared for when you feel so low. Even if you just walk every day, you will look and feel better for that next job interview. Exercise will improve your health—which will make you look and feel more confident. Look for free exercise classes in your town. Call your local hospital or clinic to find out where they are. This is another great way to meet new people and make new contacts.

Beware of over-eating or drinking. If you find yourself uncharacteristically eating ice cream bonbons or heading for your local bar, consider what's driving your behavior and be honest. You won't make new job contacts in a saloon. If you suspect that your new behavior is driven by anxiety, depression or fear, try to stop before it goes much further. If you can't seem to break this new, unhealthy problem, you should consult with a doctor. This is a very stressful time and these kinds of behaviors—while understandable—are not at all helpful. Try to remember that you don't want to start habits that will hurt you when that employment opportunity you've been waiting for comes along.

Don't forget your spiritual side. Seek comfort in meditation and prayer, and recognize that there will be an end to this. Sometimes it seems impossible to see the light at the end of the tunnel, but you have to know that it is there. Give yourself some peace by spending quiet, contemplative hours that can renew hope and confidence. Prayer and meditation about the situation, alone or with another person, can be relaxing and revitalizing. Quiet reflection about what you have done and what you can do sometimes creates a new idea. Give it a try.

No one can guarantee when you will get the job you want—or even one you don't want. You will be able to approach each day with a proactive attitude if you remind yourself that this challenging time will come to an end and that your diligence and persistence will pay off in new job situations.

New Job Strategies

Once you're no longer in your old job, usually your top priority is to get a new job. The following are some strategies you can use to help you handle this unexpected change in your career.

The résumé. You've probably been in the job market long enough to learn how to put together a résumé, so we won't spend a lot of time on this. There are some very good books out on this. However, there are a few things you can do to make sure your résumé makes the right impression.

Create a new résumé. Use the templates found in Microsoft Word or Corel's WordPerfect.

If you can afford it, have someone design your résumé for maximum effectiveness. Many small design firms and print shops will take your information and create one that is attractive without being too slick. You want to grab the attention of your intended audience. Color, type and layout can be put together to create a memorable résumé. Go back and read your information, before you start, to add new skills and experience.

Create several different résumés. If you want to stress many different skills, don't depend on one résumé to do the trick. Take the time to emphasize one aspect of your former position over others. For instance, Whitney did much of the writing and designing in her position at the event-planning firm, but she was also involved in sales. She created two different résumés highlighting the duties and accomplishments of one of those skills over the other in each one, depending on the position for which she was applying.

Treat your résumé as your ambassador. Your résumé will speak for you, so make it reader friendly and full of your positive accomplishments. Like an ambassador, it deserves dignity, not desperation; don't send it all over town to places and people you really don't have an interest in. That's a waste of time and energy for both you and the people you are sending it to.

Try sending your résumé to a few, select employers who are not advertising a job opening. Carefully choose a few companies that may have been the competition in your former job. They will know of your work by reputation and just might be flattered that you thought of them. If they don't have an opening at the moment, your résumé might spark an idea for them to put you to work!

Are you willing to relocate? Now may be the time to seek employment in another area of the country . . . or the world!

Think about new possibilities. If you have sent your résumé to all the local companies to no avail, it is time to consider another direction. Try a different field that could use your skills. Since Whitney created designs and wrote for her previous company, she could consider possibilities in advertising, travel, convention services or marketing—all of which would let her apply her skills to a new career.

Networking and Contacts. Of course you will ask your friends if they know about any job openings—but what about their friends and family? Ask everyone if they know of upcoming opportunities. Have you neglected friends from school in the last couple of years? Get in touch with them again. You'll enjoy talking to them and you can ask their advice. Would your college professors remember you? They may be able to assist you. Often they have contacts in the business community formed as part of their teaching duties.

Is It Time for a Career Change? Perhaps your job loss is an opportunity to pursue another career course. Are you ready for a whole new perspective? If you are, here is a quick check-list for you:

- Put yourself to the test. There are a lot of self-test books on the market now that can help you determine a new direction. A career counselor can also help you with career options where you can use your skills.

- Explore your options. Doing a little informal research can be beneficial. Talk to people who are working in new areas that might appeal to you. Discover if your skills would fit well into this new field. If you are interested, the person who discusses their field with you might be able to refer you. After all, they know you are available for work, open to suggestions and willing to learn.

- Start training. If you can afford to take some courses in your new career, do so. Even if you are basically qualified, training can help polish you skills even more and help you get involved in your new career. You might also get some job leads from class instructors.

- Write a strong cover letter. This is probably more important than your résumé. This letter will discuss why you want to make the move into a new career. Saying that you are moving because you didn't have a choice may be truthful, but it doesn't help your case—and it certainly won't impress a prospective employer. Use this opportunity to explain more in depth how your skills and accomplishments can translate into your new position. Show your enthusiasm for this new field.

- Volunteer your skills where they may be desperately needed. If you are good at writing, offer your services for any of a number of non-profit services. Can you answer phones, make copies, bag non-perishable food, serve soup, give a list of available services or listen to a person with empathy? Are you willing to make a long-term commitment to be a member of a board of directors for a non-profit? If this is something that interests you, you can test your skills under pressure and do a great job for people you don't know. You won't be paid but you can explore new avenues for your talents.

- Contact a temporary agency. They may be able to get you short periods of work that will enable you to pay the bills while you change careers.

- Offer to substitute for a friend or colleague who is taking time off from work to have a baby or to care for aging parents. You must understand going in the purpose of this is an opportunity for you and for the person taking the time off. It is *not* an opportunity for you to show how much better your work is for the company. That kind of reputation is one that will never leave you.

- Consider starting your own business. Go back to Chapter Ten: *Leaving the Job You Hate* and decide if owning your own business is for you.

If You Are Facing A Lay-off

Trisha, a sales rep for a national firm, had a little more warning than Whitney did. The rumors of a lay-off at her company rumbled through the media and the hallways of her corporation for months. Still, when Trisha was let go, she did not feel prepared somehow. She had only recently thought about updating her résumé, making a few contacts and considering her career options. Although Trisha would be the first to admit that she didn't especially like her job, losing it still came as a blow to her self-esteem.

First of all, be sure you are actually being laid-off. Very often, the company is firing you but calling it a lay-off. A lay-off or Reduction in Force (RIF) implies that at some point you could be rehired. Being fired means you are permanently dismissed from the company. Among other things that are affected by this difference in terminology, there are your unemployment benefits.

Like Trisha, the millions of people who have been laid-off may have disliked or even hated their jobs. Nevertheless, they experience the same sense of devastation, fear and depression that those who have been terminated feel.

Most of the information in this chapter is as relevant to the person who has been laid-off as to the one who has been fired. There are, however, a few things for the person who has been laid off to keep in mind.

Be Prepared. Trisha had the best intentions, but she didn't quite follow through on her plans once the rumors about lay-offs started. Updating a résumé, considering new career options, and networking were steps Trisha could have taken to help her advance more quickly through the jobless stage and feel more confident about being ready for changes.

Find out the Facts. You've heard the rumors. Now perhaps you can find out for sure. Nothing is more stressful than hearing bits and pieces of what might happen, conflicting announcements that may or may not apply to your department or hearing parts of conversations drifting through the corporate halls. Seek out a reliable source for the straight facts. Go to your supervisor or personnel officer and ask for any information they can give—even if it is the knowledge that you should update your résumé and try to get out ahead of the others. They may be bound by orders to keep quiet, so ask for ways you could be prepared for future unpleasant possibilities.

Think and Talk about Your Options.

Your company is considering letting you go, and you know it. Ask your supervisor to contemplate moving you into a different position within the company—if that is something that would appeal to you. If you are determined to stay with the company, would you be willing to move? Do they know you would consider a different job with them? Don't give up because of something that is happening down the road. If management is willing to listen, talk to them about what you are willing to do. Show them how you would both benefit if you stay with the firm.

Can You Become Indispensable? There is an old saying in business, that when it comes to the bottom line, no one is indispensable. In situations when the company is about to collapse, that may be true. Otherwise, there are ways to make yourself so important to your employers, that they'd never think of firing you. Try to look for new possibilities in your job.

You will recall Ann from the first chapter, who was the only one who showed interest in a terrorism training program at her company. When a terrorism specialist position opened up—an upper level job—at first, Ann didn't think she would get it. After all, two of her supervisors wanted the slot for themselves. But the woman who awarded Ann the job told her they were never seriously considered. Ann was the only one with the proper credentials, and after the events of September 11th, Ann's knowledge made her, in the supervisor's words, "indispensable." Never, ever refuse the opportunity to learn something about your job or someone else's job in your company—you never know when it may be the one thing your employer needs the most.

Acquire New Skills. In Chapter Two: *How to Fall in Love Again With Your Job,* there were suggestions about learning skills of the co-workers around you and finding a mentor. There are probably more than two or three workers in your company who have a special skill that is necessary to complete the company's product. If you are interested in learning this, offer to fill in for this person when they are sick or want to go on vacation. Approach them carefully them about their willingness to become your mentor. You don't want to make them feel that you want to take their place immediately. But there may come a day when they *do* leave that you are the only person at the company with this skill. Until then, you may become one of the few workers who has skills for more than one job. A worker who can move between positions as needed—and is willing to do so—is more valuable than one who only performs the duties in their job description. Your flexibility may well shield you from future job cuts.

Think Worst-Case Scenario. Meet your fears and anxieties head-on. By being well-prepared for the worst thing that can happen on your job, you'll gain some measure of control. Having envisioned possible problems, you can prepare the solutions in advance. Considering all the alternatives can improve your position, whatever the actual circumstances. In most cases, your worst-case scenario never materializes, so you'll be well-armed to deal with the lesser dilemmas!

Hopefully, you will never have to cope with a job loss. If you are fired, take heart! You can make it through this difficult time fortified with the strategies discussed, as well as the faith that comes from knowing that this, too, shall pass.

SPECIAL SECTION FOR EMPLOYERS

(Employees can read it too!)

" CHEER UP. I HATE YOUR JOB TOO. "

Chapter Twelve

How to Love the Employee You Hate

To: Jesus, Son of Joseph
            Wood Crafter Carpenter Shop
            Nazareth 25922
From: Jordan Management Consultants
            Jerusalem 26544
            Re: Results of Personality Evaluations

Thank you for submitting the résumés of the twelve men you have selected for management positions in your new organization. All have taken our battery of tests. We have run their results through our computer. Evaluations were made from personal interviews with our psychologist and our vocational aptitude consultant. We are enclosing the profiles of each test and urge you to review them carefully.

In addition to our regular reports, we are also presenting a few general comments derived from our staff consultants and evaluations on some of the nominees. There is no additional cost for this service.

It is our considered opinion that most of your nominees are seriously lacking in background, education and vocational aptitude for your enterprise, as we understand it. They do not show any evidence of having a "team concept," an essential trait. Frankly, we recommend that you continue your search for capable persons who have had relevant experience and who can demonstrate management skills and capabilities.

Simon Peter is emotionally unstable, showing fits of temper and accompanying irrationality.

Andrew is entirely devoid of leadership ability.

The brothers James and John, the sons of Zebedee, apparently place their personal interests above company loyalty.

Thomas exhibits an attitude of questioning and disbelief, something certain to undermine morale.

We also feel you should be aware that Matthew has been officially blacklisted by the Greater Jerusalem Better Business Bureau, apparently for good cause.

James, son of Alpheus, and Thaddeus showed definite radical tendencies, as well as achieving inordinately high scores on the manic-depressive scale.

However, one of your candidates shows great potential. He is a man of ability and great resourcefulness, seems to be truly people-oriented, shows excellent business acumen, and has contacts in high places. He tested as being highly motivated, ambitious and responsible. We would recommend that Judas Iscariot become your controller, if not your most trusted associate.

All other profiles are self-explanatory. We wish you every success in your new venture.

Sincerely yours,

The Jordan Management Group

—Anonymous

There are tests to evaluate potential employees and analyze everything from intelligence to sales ability. You can go over a résumé or job application with extreme care. You can check references from previous employers and personal acquaintances. Yet, you can still end up with an employee who drives you crazy for a multitude of reasons. So why do you still end up with personnel who look good on paper but end up being difficult? Well, they are people! And very often people have areas that need a little work.

First, it helps to know there is a problem. It is a lot more cost-effective to solve that problem than it is to go through hiring and training employees until you find that gem who wants your company to succeed as much—if not more—than you do. The smart employer will make it a point to know the workers he or she has hired, and will invest in the development of their skills and talents to get their best possible work. The result is more than a win-win working environment; it is greater profit.

The purpose of this chapter is to explore several areas that are potential causes for difficulties with employees, including simple discipline problems. The most important message underlying all of these is that, in an uncertain economy, an employer does not have the luxury of replacing employees who are not reaching their potential productivity. Here are some common difficulties and thoughts on handling them:

The Generation Gap and the Changing Employee

If you are an older supervisor with a younger employee, you may experience some exasperation with differing values of your younger workers. That is natural, as each generation tends to have different goals and lifestyles.

Baby Boomers, who are now in supervisory positions with many years of experience, report the highest job satisfaction of any generation group. Having ridden the waves of economic and societal changes, they are looking forward to passing their knowledge and experience to the next generation of workers. Many can't understand a younger worker who is not grateful for a steady job with a strong company. They have a hard time empathizing with someone who challenges the corporate culture over what they perceive as petty problems. I've heard many employers ask the same question, "Don't they like prosperity?" Between the generations, prosperity is in the eye of the beholder.

Later generations tend to be a much more cynical and ambitious group. More recent age groups are not as willing to be patient in seeking advancement and career goals. One can accuse this cohort of having a common thought—"We want it all and we want it now." Try to remember you may have felt this way yourself at one time.

Younger employees need clearly defined work environments. Be specific about what is wanted from them and why. Give them concrete rewards—though not necessarily money. Days off, vacations, stereos can go a long way to boosting morale. Provide short-term goals and show how achieving those will build to a successful career in the company. Most are hard workers and are just looking for the right motivation.

And after all, they may not share your sense of loyalty to the company. Some, seeing what they perceive as a better opportunity, will leave your employ despite your good management. This is not necessarily a reflection on you or the company, but a more practical approach to jobs in general.

Use honesty and trust to build a relationship with them that encourages their ambition and your shared success. Let them know that you don't demand their loyalty but want to earn it by sharing your work triumphs with them. They can be building a great résumé for those greener pastures, when the opportunity presents itself by working hard for you. Make it clear that you are willing to be a partner in their career path, and follow through by sharing any credit for successful projects with them.

If you are a younger supervisor with an older worker, you may have to deal with the reverse problem. Older workers often resent being told what to do and how to do it by younger bosses who may not have half as much experience as they do. A manager who is sensitive to this natural tendency can usually overcome it by treating older workers with the respect they deserve for their experience and accomplishments. Avoid automatically labeling them in your mind as "outdated." These employees can provide you with a wealth of insight gathered from a lot more living. Be willing to listen to their perspective.

Showing empathy for their experience will gain their trust and give you the value of their knowledge. Both of you will win, as they will have your support, and they will give you a certain amount of mentoring that may be missing in your company life. This is a rare opportunity for both of you.

Behavioral Disabilities

Sheila was promoted to manager of a staff of three architects in a small commercial design firm. From the beginning, she was aware that Kevin—the brightest and most talented architect, despite his youth—could sometimes be a handful. She assigned him the projects that required innovative thinking and she was usually rewarded with satisfied clients.

While another architect was on an extended vacation, Sheila assigned Kevin a project for a client who was a bit more conservative than he was used to handling. When he presented his first set of plans, she knew they were too modern and the client would not accept them. She explained to Kevin that his work was excellent but he needed to make some revisions to accommodate the client. Kevin became sullen and uncooperative, arguing that his plans were fine. Then he began to complain about the client. His behavior quickly escalated to just short of a temper tantrum before he stomped off to his office to sulk.

Stunned by his behavior, Sheila asked the others in the office if this was Kevin's usual behavior. There were indications—though no one would come right out and say it—that it was. She checked his file and discovered that he had been reprimanded a few times by his former supervisor, but no action had been taken.

Sheila made an appointment to talk privately with Kevin. She discovered that he felt very badly about his behavior. He readily admitted to having a long history of having problems with frustration. After some careful questioning, Sheila began to suspect that Kevin had other issues that even he was not aware of.

She assured him that he was a valuable employee whose talent and dedication she did not want to lose. She suggested he get professional counseling and testing to find out if there was treatment for the lack of self-confidence in his work. Kevin sincerely wanted to keep his job and readily agreed to the counseling and testing. Through a waiver, he assented to having his counselor share the results with Sheila.

After several sessions with a psychologist and some diagnostic testing, the mystery was solved. Kevin was identified as having a condition called Attention Deficit Disorder (ADD). This is a learning disability most commonly associated with children. Left untreated, however, people who suffer from ADD often repeat patterns of failure throughout their adult lives.

Kevin received medication to help control the ADD and learned, in a relatively short period of time, how to control his emotional outbursts. Because the medication lessened the frustration over his inability to stay focused, his organizational skills improved right away. He had been working three times as hard as his colleagues to produce the same work, in the past. Suddenly, he found his job a thrill.

Had Sheila handled Kevin in the traditional manner, she might have fired a valuable and talented employee. But she recognized that Kevin's talent and personality were worth the extra effort. Sheila's professional and compassionate handling of his personality made him her most loyal and valuable employee. His designs have since won several national awards for the firm and many new, prestigious clients due to his reputation.

The moral of this story is that a problem employee may actually be turned into an opportunity. But this can only happen if managers and supervisors are willing to look beyond the standards that are applied to most people.

The Personality Clash

If you find your problem with the employee is a difference in personalities, go back in this book and reread Chapter Three: *How to Love the Personality You Hate*. Remember to analyze whether someone is being rebellious or just acting out the inclinations of a their temperament. Does the employee seem to be too nit-picky, or is it the attention to minutia that comes naturally to a detail-person? Perhaps you are exasperated about a person who exhibits a lack of focus. Would their behavior make more sense if you understood that you are dealing with an outgoing, sociable people-person? Or maybe it troubles you that a worker seems quiet and meek. Realizing that a support-person never complains about doing extra work and always has a pleasant attitude may help you adjust your opinion.

The key to resolving personality clashes is to remember that what bothers you most in another person may just be the strength you lack and need the most. The next time that gregarious people-person gets on your nerves, try sending him out to charm your most frustrating client. You'll learn to appreciate his talent for schmoozing!

The point of all of this is that you, the employer, should begin to look at your employees as company assets. While each has a different personality trait that can make you crazy, each one of them also has a unique talent. You don't want a team built with the same personality traits. You would not get the diverse talents that enhance the culture of your company. Don't you think your taxes need to be done by a person who lives for details? I'd want someone like that reviewing any contract I might sign. While that meek and mild support-person is alone in her office designing a new advertising campaign, spend time with her. Listen to every aspect of the project as she describes it—stifling your desire to interrupt—so that you, a people-person, can nail the presentation to the client.

It's also a good investment to have a solid people-person as a receptionist. A good receptionist can win a new client for you just by answering the phone. They can turn a tentative inquiry into an enthusiastic business client. While you are on another line, your receptionist could strike up a conversation, instead of hitting that "hold" button. A really great receptionist can also be a gold mine for bits of important information about your clients that might help the detail-person design the best proposal for them.

While your command-person employee may not get along with a support-person staff member, partner them together to plan and execute a big project. Remind them that they have very different strengths, and if they can get past that to create a big project, it would be quite an achievement for both of them. The same way that different traits complement each other, your employees can balance the strengths and weaknesses of their co-workers and you, if you foster that kind of working environment.

There's Always One Rotten Apple

No matter how many wonderful employees you are blessed with over time, there is bound to be one or two who are downright incorrigible. They are the discipline problems that refuse to respond to any amount of fair treatment, second chances or disciplinary actions.

Ellen was a recent college graduate seeking a job in a television station. She wanted to be a reporter, believing that her college journalism courses and internships had prepared her well. Ellen also wanted quick advancement and immediate rewards.

She found an opening in a small station as a secretary and took the job, hoping to move into a reporter position as soon as possible. Though Ellen was an excellent worker, her abrasive style and obvious contempt for the secretarial job became a problem for her boss and co-workers. Ellen was politely asked on several occasions to be more patient and courteous with clients. But her frustration with the job grew, and she began to refuse even fifteen minutes of over-time to finish typing an important letter.

Her boss finally set up a meeting to discuss her situation. He assured Ellen that he understood her desire to move into news reporting, but asked her to understand that he needed her in her current job. He also pointed out that her lack of dedication to this job could indicate she was not ready to take on more responsibility.

Ellen angrily quit without even giving two week's notice. The station was left without a replacement, and a great deal of chaos ensued until she could be replaced.

Ellen then began a bout of job-hopping among small suburban newspapers and radio stations. At each she was fired for her unreliability and uncooperative attitude. She is a truly capable worker and may even be an excellent reporter someday. However, at this stage of her life, she has obviously not developed sufficient maturity to deal with the demands of a job.

An employer avoids the chaos Ellen left in her wake by writing a job description that is very specific and makes no promises for advancement. If you advertise for a secretarial job opening, then you should stick to the needs of your company and be very careful to hire the applicant who wants that job. Note that the jobs Ellen found were for small companies that probably didn't have many opportunities for advancement. Her lack of maturity and sophistication probably set her up to fail at her job, but the person who hired her may have set the company up for the eventual discord.

Employers beware. Be clear about your needs when you hire. Any misinterpreted or implied promises of possible advancement can be dangerous.

Handling the Problem Employee

Before you deal with a problem employee, it is best to have a clear and concise Policies and Procedures manual. If you don't have a manual and you have one or more employees, create one. It can be very simple and held together with a staple. Don't delay. Some companies call their agreement a Standard Operating Procedures (SOP) booklet or Employee Handbook. Your company Policies and Procedures manual is just a list of expectations between you and those who are employed by you. When an employee is hired, their first duty should be to sit down and read the manual. Then they should sign a statement that they did so. That agreement goes in their personnel file and they can keep the manual.

You should be very clear about how an employee would be fired. There should be a standard process with the employee getting a chance to be heard or have advocacy. Your responsibility to your employees must include your written feedback, or constructive criticism, listing how you support improvement. The best form of documented feedback, from employer to employee, is the performance evaluation. There are many forms available, but this is such an important tool for employers that I have written an entire chapter on the subject. For more information about evaluations, read Chapter Fourteen: *How to Love the Performance Evaluations We All Hate.*

As an employer, you need to address problems as soon as you are made aware of them. It's not fair to allow negative behavior to continue. Your reaction must be calm and consistent with all employees. If you are a supervisor, you can discuss the problem employee with someone in the personnel office—if you have one—or another supervisor. Make a plan and set an appointment to speak privately with the employee. No matter how busy you are, don't put it off. While it is wise to plan on the meeting when both you and the employee aren't angry or defensive, don't make it for the following week, causing tension and worry for everyone who is waiting for the resolution.

The most effective method is to meet with the employee and explain the specific undesirable behavior or weakening performance. Talk about the implications and possible consequences of the problems. Offer support—both instructional and emotional—to help the employee correct them. Invite the employee to explain, from his or her perspective, why the problems are occurring. Then listen.

Ask questions about the possibility of a stressful situation in their personal life. Offer resources to counsel and support the employee. Ask for feedback on your management techniques and find out if you could be more helpful.

Assure the employee he is valuable to the organization. Your goal is to see him succeed, not to punish or embarrass him. Stress you measure your success by the success of your subordinates; that you want to work with him to turn the situation around. Set a specific time—say a week or two—when both of you will meet again to see if there are positive differences in the problem.

If there is denial from the employee about his or her responsibility for the problem, then you need to let them know that you will investigate the issue, because there has to be a resolution to the problem. Ask if there are co-workers who can substantiate his statements. One way or the other, be clear on the timeline you have given for the negative behavior to stop. Inform the employee that if there is continued improvement, he can consider this a verbal warning. The two of you should agree on simple objectives for the employee that can be measured by your next meeting.

At the next meeting, if there are signs that the employee is trying to meet the objectives, you are both on the road to resolving the situation. However, if it is fairly obvious that no effort has been made to meet them, you should probably begin probationary warnings, according to your company's personnel policies and procedures. Bring a memo to the meeting, referring to the specific policy, and ask them to sign a copy of the written probationary warning. They should be allowed to write their comments, as they wish, on the memo and then place the memo in their personnel file. Make sure that you have spelled out exactly what behavior or non-compliance there is to warrant the action that could result in termination.

In terms of your time, losing a team member you have trained, searching for a new employee and the general tension in your workforce when someone is fired, you can't afford termination. Effort must be directed toward your present workers to maximize their productivity and guard your profits. By working with your employee, you will create trust, which will spur him or her on to work harder for you. Both you and your personnel can work together to realize your highest potential of *team self-esteem*—which will impact your bottom line directly.

CHAPTER THIRTEEN
ADDRESSING YOUR EMPLOYEES' NEEDS

In a perfect world, employers wouldn't have to worry about workers' feelings, stress, health and other issues. Employees would simply come in to work and give their best performance to achieve superior productivity for your business. But it rarely works out that way, does it? Each worker comes to you with their own range of "issues." How—and if—you cope with those situations can make the difference between having a high turn-over rate and a group of loyal employees willing to give you their all.

In this chapter, we will touch on some of the many difficulties your employees face. Then I will address some of the ways to deal with these situations in a way that will help you have a healthy, productive employee.

Stress

You need to make sure your workplace environment is not so tension-filled that it fosters addiction and other negative coping behaviors. This is often hard in an age of cutbacks and work force reductions. There is a fine line between pressing for better productivity and expecting your employees to work long hours for little pay just to slice a thin margin of profit.

Is morale so low and tension so high that your employees are stress-related accidents or illnesses waiting to happen? What can you do about it, besides continuing to buy more insurance at higher costs that eat away your profit? Insurance premiums increase when your carrier finds your workers are more susceptible to stress-related maladies. Be aware of how the work environment is affecting your employees—and you as well.

Stress manifests itself in many ways, as discussed in Chapter Nine: *How to Love the Stress You Hate.* Here are some of the problems your employees may develop in a stressful environment:

Absenteeism. The National Center for Health Statistics shows that for every hundred employees, employers will lose about ten months of workdays per year to sickness and injuries. If an employer has added increased tension and stress due to cutbacks and cost-cutting measures, the loss in productivity will rapidly increase. Every employer knows the collateral costs for every worker who is out of his job. Other workers must pick up the slack, adding those duties to their own. If the workforce has already been reconfigured to compensate for reductions in personnel, absenteeism due to sick leave begins to eat away at good customer service and the quality and quantity of the business product. Once your workforce begins to go down that road, it's almost impossible to get them back on track.

Mental Illness and Addictions

Stress at work or at home, low self-esteem or simple chemical imbalances can make your employees dependent on drugs, alcohol and other addictive behavior in an attempt to cope. They also have a greater tendency to experience mental and emotional health problems, such as depression, that require some form of professional treatment. Managers need to learn to look for signs of problems and deal with them pro-actively and compassionately.

Depression. Jana worked at a medium-sized direct mail company for about three years. She was a database manager for some large national clients and was an excellent worker. Her boss, Michael, considered her a star in his company. However, over time, Michael began to notice Jana seemed bored and disinterested in the work she used to love. She forgot things that had been clearly spelled out in meetings, turned in reports that lacked detail and often left the office at five o'clock sharp, or even a few minutes earlier. In meetings, she was unusually quiet and contributed little in brainstorming sessions. When questioned about ideas or plans for her clients, Jana responded with skepticism. Her enthusiasm had waned. It seemed Jana felt that it was not worth her effort to come up with any new plans or ideas.

From the first time he interviewed her, Michael knew that, given her the skills and by sharing his experience with her, Jana could be the best employee he had ever hired. Michael invested a lot of training dollars in Jana and was rewarded by her performance and productivity. During a bad economic slowdown—when Michael was worried he might have to close the business—Jana took over some of his duties for him. It was her loyalty and drive that got her co-workers through that six-month period—which ended in unexpected profit. Michael felt indebted to her and cared about her well-being.

One day, Michael went into Jana's office and sat down across from her. He quietly said, "Jana, you seem like the most unhappy person on earth. Life is too short for you to be so sad. I want to know what's wrong and what I can do to help."

Jana was stunned, thinking she had kept her feelings well hidden. But she was touched by Michael sincere desire to help her. She was surprised at how easily her feelings came tumbling out. She told Michael she had lost the ability to feel motivated in all areas of her life, not just work. She feared she might be suffering from depression and in need of a psychiatrist, but worried that if she went for treatment, someone would find out. She was embarrassed by the idea being of mentally ill. Jana was convinced her co-workers wouldn't want to work with someone with her problems.

Michael assured her he supported her desire for counseling and whole-heartedly encouraged her to seek the best psychologist she could find. He promised total confidentiality about her problems and offered to help her in any way at work the counselor might suggest. His management style of showing empathy and going to her office instead of calling her in to his—she would surely have felt she was being called "on the carpet" for something negative—saved a valuable employee. Michael's support and encouragement allowed Jana to get the help she needed. Within six weeks she was back on track, giving her clients her very best work.

Unfortunately, many people have incorrect ideas about depression. As discussed in Chapter Eight: *How to Love the Stress You Hate,* depression lasting more than a couple of weeks is cause to seek professional help. As many as fifteen million Americans suffer from clinical depression; some may not realize it. Because society treats it with such prejudice, people are often afraid to seek help for fear of being labeled mentally ill or emotionally unstable.

The employee who appears driven to succeed is often the one you have to watch. Clinical depression is serious, but it is also treatable. Make sure your company's health insurance covers some type of mental or emotional health coverage. Additionally, you should have a counseling program available.

Drug and alcohol addiction. Firing addicted employees is an expensive way to deal with this problem, since the cost of recruiting and training new staff is increasing every year. Doing so may also violate the Americans with Disabilities Act of 1992. Prevention, or even addressing drug and alcohol addiction in the early stages, can save employers a lot of money and salvage valuable employees. The cost of treating addictions is actually far less than treating medical problems that result from them. Studies show the daily cost of medical care for chemical dependence is less than half that of treating illnesses such as cirrhosis, high blood pressure, strokes, ulcers, and trauma (accidents) resulting from untreated addictions.

Workaholism. An addictive personality can just as easily be addicted to his or her job, making great productivity a part of who they believe they are. While such a worker may seem beneficial for the company, it can lead to that employee becoming burned-out or induce stress-related illness. Then the company would lose that valuable worker—and perhaps their family would lose a loved one as well. Help your employees maintain a reasonable work schedule with enough time off to take part in the rest of their lives. No employer can afford to have a key worker who has an unhealthy balance in his life. All work and no play *makes Jack sick.*

Self-Esteem

If you haven't already, please read Chapter Eight: *How to Love Yourself* on this subject. Workers with low self-esteem cannot produce at their top capacity. Poor self-image will prevent employees from coping with new systems, hardware and procedures. They will have difficulty interacting with other workers. Stress combined with poor self-esteem will make their work even more difficult.

Domestic Violence Is a Workplace Issue

Domestic violence often follows an employee into the workplace. One out of every four American women has been abused by a husband or boyfriend. (Although there are cases of men being abused, this is a much smaller group.) Most of them are working women. In my forthcoming book *Surviving Him: How to Stay Out Once You Get Out* I address the signs and symptoms of domestic violence as it affects the workplace:

- She will be consistently late to work. . . always with a different excuse.

- She will appear shaky, distracted and nervous. Her hands may tremble.

- She will not be as productive.

- There will be increased, unexplained, medical expenses.

- She may seem anxious, depressed and tearful.

- She may avoid people at work, so that she is not forced to answer any questions.

The abused person may show most or a few of these signs.

What can a manager do to help? First, address the abuse indirectly. Ask open-ended questions that allow the employee to engage in dialogue. Because of today's current legal and privacy climate, she must volunteer the information. The employee has to know that you care enough to listen and that you will keep it confidential. Show that you will offer her support and information. And just listen.

What can your company or organization do to help? Create an awareness of how rampant domestic violence is. Don't be afraid to talk about it. It is one of the best kept secrets in America. Until we bring it out, this tragedy will continue to perpetuate itself. Your organization should have policies to ensure the workplace is a safe and responsive place for employees seeking help. There is so much shame and fear attached to domestic violence that if a woman feels the company will not provide support, she may continue to suffer in silence.

Countless companies across the country are recognizing that responding to domestic violence is "good business." The following is a checklist that employers can use to address domestic violence in their workplaces:

- Hold training seminars that include how to recognize and discuss with all staff members workplace policies regarding domestic violence.

- Post the number for the National Domestic Violence Hotline: 1-800-799-SAFE on your employee bulletin board.

- Provide counseling, publicize your Employee Assistance Program and / or local domestic violence programs.

- Include frequent articles about domestic violence in your company newsletter detailing the company's policies.

- Display posters with anti-domestic violence information.

- Make changes to improve security. Something as simple as providing a photograph of the batterer can save a life.

- Assign one well-trained and compassionate staff member to address domestic violence issues.

- Connect your company's response to a larger community-wide movement. For example, you may get involved in lobbying efforts to enact domestic violence legislation.

- Lastly, remember there's never an excuse for domestic violence. We often hear, "It always takes two." In domestic violence, it only takes one. It's all about power and control. If we want to stop the cycle of abuse, we need to be a part of the solution. Everyone can do something to help.

Physical Disabilities

There is a group of people who are thrilled to be working, find joy in being among the gainfully employed and are usually the most loyal staff an employer can find. These are people who are physically disabled—or challenged, as many prefer to call themselves. The Americans with Disabilities Act, passed in 1992, requires employers with fifteen or more workers to make reasonable accommodations to hire qualified disabled persons. Have you had the opportunity to consider hiring a disabled worker? Have you examined your beliefs about how that would or would not benefit your company?

The Department of Labor and the Government Accounting Office has estimated that half of all workers with disabilities can be employed with changes that cost less than fifty dollars. If you have reservations about working with disabled employees, consider that the costs are minor compared to the benefits.

Think of your most valuable employee. Now imagine arriving at your office one morning and discovering that this person has been in an automobile accident. It seems natural that you would rush to the hospital to assure them that their job and benefits are not a problem. Suppose, after they recovered, your employee is mentally and emotionally as good as he or she ever was—but has a physical disability. Your choice is either to build a wheelchair ramp and move some office furniture to accommodate your employee, or fire them and spend time and money getting someone else who might be less valuable to you.

The answer is what they call a "no-brainer," isn't it? A disabled worker is no different from anyone else. They just need a little accommodation from you and your company.

Literacy and Basic Skills

Some researchers estimate that more than twenty million American workers are functionally illiterate. Yet managers prefer to spend their education and training dollars on leadership and computer training. Few employers have been willing to partner with non-profit groups to offer literacy programs at the work site.

With the large influx of immigrants into the work force, businesses must be prepared to help meet the educational needs of those who need to overcome economic, cultural and language barriers. There is a serious need to offer, subsidize and encourage more basic skills training. Those at the lower levels of the organization must be included in these programs because this is the employee pool from which you'll discover, motivate and train your future stars.

Consider the advantage of hiring a worker who you can economically train. When you help someone who is willing to learn, you improve both of your situations. You'll be gaining a valuable employee who is able to communicate in your company. They'll have new confidence and a better understanding of how best to do their job better.

Working with Your Employees

Trust is difficult to achieve. Managers fear vulnerability, loss of control and authority, conflict and disagreement. That is why many companies have preferred to manage by numbers or quotas, rather than building trust and teamwork.

Put Teams to Work for Your Business. If trust exists between management and employees, workers will feel comfortable putting forth their ideas about their best work product. The concept is as old as choosing a team of the strongest horses to pull a stagecoach from point A to point B.

Management's new role is to find the best people and build teams that will work together. Employers must recognize their workers' achievements. The success of the business should be credited to the ideas and hard work of the employees. Managers must motivate them with training that makes their jobs easier. Creating pride in their work product is essential to creating group self-esteem. And finally, tangible and intangible rewards help to make goal attainment that much more worthwhile.

Supervisors should empower the teams by allowing employees to make decisions, support those choices and the team's effort to achieve goals. Encourage employees to see the company as their own—so that its success is in their best interest. While it is important for management to provide direction, it is equally valuable to listen to employees' ideas and facilitate team meetings to achieve the goals of the company.

Once the team is motivated to see a project through to the end, the group must be given the tools they need to carry it out. These can be as varied as their ideas for a project. There are business consultants and speakers (like me) who teach team building skills to business managers. Sometimes a facilitator is needed who can assign project tasks to appropriately skilled team members. This is where it is important to know each of your employees and their individual capabilities. Use that knowledge to get the best that each of your employees can give. To complete your project you may need to move workers to different departments or reconfigure your workplace to facilitate teamwork. Consult with your employees. They may have ideas about colleagues in other departments who can help all of you achieve your goals.

Develop a mission statement and ask employees to refine it. Thoroughly examine your market. Study how your products and services address them. Determine a long-term vision for your company or department that will place you in the position of having the most profitable solution for those needs. Consider all your company's resources for fulfilling those needs—especially your human resources. Now, mold this new vision of what your business can be into a clearly defined path to your business goal. Make your vision as specific and vivid as possible so that all of your employees can embrace it as their own.

Plan a "company vision day" and hire an effective speaker from outside your firm. Have your employees come to work dressed comfortably. You can meet at a park or recreation center. Bring simple food or sack lunches. Do your best to have your employees relaxed and feeling open to a new idea—and that is that you want them to help you build a vision of your business.

You can have them try to improve on your mission statement. Or, you can set your own mission statement aside and see what your employees come up with. You could be in for a shock. They may have an entirely different view on the company's goals. It is important that you know if your employees are on the same page as you are. Give them the opportunity to show you what they feel they are capable of under your management and given your resources.

If your mission statement is considerably different from the one your workers develop, make sure they feel comfortable about being open and honest with their input. This will give your complainers the opportunity to be heard. You can discard what is irrelevant. Encourage all of your employees to offer their ideas, particularly the bold concepts that can excite your workforce to carry your company into new areas of success. Be open to new opportunities. The ideas that come with a small measure of risk may be worth pursuing—especially if your employees are willing to share that peril with you. Whether you blend your mission statement with your employees, or theirs with yours, complete your company mission statement, publish it, and make sure everyone gets a copy of it.

When the economy is sluggish and the future seems more uncertain than usual, you may want to periodically meet with your employees to reexamine your mission statement. You don't have to be stuck with a one that has not kept up or has become irrelevant. Repeat the process of teaming up with your company to create a mission statement at regular intervals. It is such a great motivator for your employees—and for you!

Conduct regular employee surveys. There are many outside consultants who will conduct an impartial survey of your company's workers and present the information in a detailed analysis. Most management consultants recommend doing these surveys periodically.

If employers choose, surveys can be an anonymous way to adjust weak management skills in various departments. It can provide the employer with the types of training that may be needed. Your workers can safely point out efficiency flaws in production without fears of reprisals. The simple question, "how can we improve in this area?" can lead to better products and services or cost-saving measures in the company. Some companies run a customer satisfaction survey at the same time, to examine similarities between what your employees can do better, and what your customers want to be better. I've been amazed at simple, low-cost changes that some of the surveys triggered. The result is higher profit. Those that involved customer satisfaction increased employee pride in their job. The employer gets a win all the way around.

Institute a vigorous program of education and self-improvement. The more you invest in employees' development, the less you will have to invest in other more expensive costs, such as lost sales, lower productivity, turnover, rehiring and stress related illness and injuries.

Earlier in this chapter, I discussed the immigrant employee who may not have good literacy skills. But many businesses are finding that immigrants are also consumers. It makes sense to hire a bilingual worker to communicate with your Spanish-speaking customers—or whatever language your customers are speaking. Hiring a second language tutor, especially for your workers who interact with customers is one of the better investments an employer can make in this global economy.

Another strategy for your training investment is to utilize your best employees as team mentors for newly-hired trainees. You probably have a few great employees who love what they do and know all the ins and outs of their job. Instead of thrusting this new person into a job and expecting them to fit in to your company right away, your team mentors will assure that the transition for that person into the company's culture is a smooth one.

Think about designing your own apprenticeship program with input and participation from those great employees described above. The Federal Job Training Partnership Act provides funds for businesses to hire applicants who have no experience and have not had the opportunity to get the experience. This partnership identifies workers who need a chance. They are given basic skills training and basic work ethic education. The JTPA was formed with the recognition that business owners cannot afford to hire and pay wages and benefits while employees learn entry-level skills. This program can be the boost a company and a community need to get back in the game, after an economic slump. If you want workers trained to do the job your way, and you have employees who know their job well enough to train others, give your local JTPA office a call.

Whether you design your own apprenticeship program or partner with one that exists, think about hiring someone with a real interest in your field, who is looking for a chance to work hard and learn. He may not have an extensive résumé, but he should be able to offer references from former teachers, coaches, a minister or community leader. If your new hire agrees to attend the classes, pay for them. Night classes at your local community college are inexpensive and taught by people who have been successful in their field.

If you take the time to ask your employees what they need to do a better job for you, your reward will be swift in coming. They know exactly what they lack in skills and knowledge to be more productive.

Drive out fear. In my experience, nothing brings about depression and burnout in a worker more quickly than fear. This has to be the most powerful distraction to productivity any business will face.

Management must create an emotional atmosphere where people are secure enough to ask tough questions and to ask for help when they need it. They must not be afraid of losing their jobs if they do so. This is essential to developing trust. The key is for managers to learn how to ask for honest feedback and facilitate communication. Managers should strive to understand their employees' work and personal needs. They must value workers' participation in running the company. When fear is reduced, trust is built. Satisfaction and commitment are increased.

Offer all the support programs you can for your employees. Whatever kinds of support programs you can provide to help employees cope with the stress of the daily work environment will greatly benefit the company. It is far cheaper to institute wellness programs, stress-management programs, Employee Assistance Programs, employee satisfaction surveys, and self-improvement programs than to pay the staggering costs that result when no such programs are available.

CHAPTER FOURTEEN
PERFORMANCE EVALUATIONS WE ALL HATE

As many as thirty million white collar careers will either hit the fast track or derail this year as a result of one of the most dreaded work experiences: the performance review. Whether giving or getting reviews, both managers and staffers find the experience uncomfortable. Hard economic times make evaluations even more stressful, as they may be viewed as harbingers of job loss.

Even if there were no formal performance evaluations, you would still find yourself appraising others and being appraised. It is human nature to judge, even if it's only a thought such as: *She's so organized, I know I can always count on her,* or, *He certainly seems willing, but he doesn't follow through.*

If every performance evaluation was done well, it would not be such a dreaded experience! Reviews should be used to highlight accomplishments, identify areas of improvement and set goals for the future. But they aren't always, are they? The most important thing for supervisors to remember is performance reviews are not an opportunity to bludgeon employees for their inadequacies or take revenge for irritating behavior. If reviews are used as punitive devices, they will not only be ineffective, but may actually aggravate problem situations by fostering resentment.

What follows are some of the potential problems related to performance evaluations:

- Even though it's human nature to judge, it is also human nature to resist being judged.

- It is often difficult for supervisors to be frank in their criticism when they want their group or division to appear in the best light.

- Some supervisors are very uncomfortable giving criticism and so they don't do it well—or do not do it at all. This robs both the employee and the employer of an opportunity to improve performance.

- In some cases, the relationship between the supervisor and worker is damaged by the evaluation.

- Management rarely gives priority to performance evaluations, often putting them off as long as possible. Again, the chance to maximize worker productivity is greatly lessened.

- One research study disclosed that only 30 percent of twenty-five thousand employees found their personal performance rating effective in giving them information about their own work.

- Another survey found that 40 percent of employees never knew they'd been evaluated.

The performance evaluation is an opening for both the reviewer and the employee to help each other. By working together as a team, they can find ways to enhance their abilities. The supervisor is in a position to encourage the employee, and in the process, he may even help himself. We can adapt the Golden Rule to read: Help your workers do their jobs, as you would want your workers to help you do your job (or run your business).

Creating the Right Tone for Communication

The key word is empowerment. It is a mutual effort. You each have a chance to communicate what works, what doesn't and how to make it work better. It is up to the supervisor to set up a review-friendly environment in which the employee doesn't feel intimidated. Even if there are problems to be addressed, the worker must feel valued in order to overcome the natural resistance to being judged.

Reviewers need to evaluate themselves in relation to each employee. They must consider their attitude toward the worker, his or her personality, work style and values. Supervisors should consider their own personality, work style, values and relationship with the employee. Care must be taken that an employee is not unfairly evaluated according to the personality and style of the supervisor, instead of that of the employee. In other words, a support-person should not be evaluated as a command-person, or a people-person as a detail person. Evaluate the staff member according to the best of his or her abilities, not yours.

Empowerment also means it is the supervisor's job to create an environment that makes people want to perform. It is up to the employee to communicate what is needed for such an atmosphere and follow through with the promised performance, when that environment is provided. The performance evaluation then becomes a two-way street, allowing both parties to determine how well they have lived up to their bargain, or whether some aspect of it needs revision.

Prior to an evaluation, both reviewer and employee need to prepare. The reviewer needs to know the employee's working abilities before the review process begins. The worker needs to do a self-evaluation, prioritizing strengths, listing plans for overcoming any weaknesses, and imagining future potential. Some companies allow the employee to fill out a blank copy of the review form for comparison with that of their supervisor.

One human resources manager I've spoken with suggests an on-going review process with periodic reviews leading up to an annual evaluation. Informal discussions should continue throughout the year to review changes in expectations and business objectives.

A manager of regional hospital employees strongly recommends quarterly evaluations. Waiting for the annual review can allow unproductive work habits to become ingrained. Quarterly reviews also eliminate the element of surprise if a negative evaluation must be given. This method helps the employee to strengthen his or her work habits.

Another crucial element for both reviewer and employee is the ability to listen. Interruptions should be prevented so that both parties can concentrate on hearing what is said and understanding each other. If a statement is unclear, neither person should hesitate to ask for clarification. It is advisable to take notes so that specific points can be referred to later for further discussion or amplification. Open dialog should be encouraged to make the process less judgmental and more of a team effort. The process is only effective when both reviewer and employee can respond appropriately to each other.

A Look at Various Appraisal Systems

Trait System: If your company has a form that asks you to rate employees on a scale (usually one to five) according to such criteria as "works well with others" or "punctual," and so on, it is using a trait evaluation system—the oldest form of performance evaluation. The trait system, however, does not consider the content of a job.

Behavior Anchored Rating Scales (BARS): This method is well-suited to evaluating large numbers of employees who do the same job, such as cashiers or bank tellers. Degrees of competence in observable job behaviors are measured. The benefit of BARS is that it reduces subjectivity and inconsistency. The downside is it focuses too much attention on what the employee does, not on the outcome.

Management by Objective (MBO): The employee states in advance what he or she expects to accomplish on the job in the coming six months or year. Supervisors help the employee set up a plan for improving performance and accomplishing their goals. This evaluation approach is based on outcome rather than behavior or traits. Accountability is more precise and goal oriented. A series of milestones may be determined for the employee to work toward in a given period of time. This is the most accepted system for judging managers.

Critical Incidents Log: In each employee's file, managers keep anecdotal information on accomplishments and other significant events. This is consistent with the current tendency toward less rigid kinds of evaluations and more open-ended methods of assessing workers.

Finding a "Perfect Ten": This system employs a comparison guide to analyze performance. People are promoted not because they achieve specific objectives but rather because they achieve better than others do.

Mutual Assessment: A current approach to performance evaluations recruits staffers in the practice of assessing one another and measuring the supervisory process. It is hoped that this peer-to-peer rating and subordinate-boss approach will make for a less intimidating, more nurturing method.

Self-assessment: This is also encouraged more and more, with the desired end being more emphasis on personal growth. This type of evaluation provides a reliable indicator of where the worker feels they are in his or her career. Filling out an evaluation form prior to a review allows employees to develop an understanding of their own expectations, accomplishments and future plans.

Consider these questions

- Examine your company's evaluation system. Does it fall into one of the above categories?

- How is it used?

- Who sees it?

- Does it determine bonuses, promotions, or raises?

- How could it be designed better, and used as a tool for you to get the optimum potential from your employees?

- How could it be used to help supervisors and subordinates do their jobs better?

- How can it give you information about how best you invest in employee training, for example?

- What weaknesses do you see identified throughout your company that you can make stronger with one training plan?

Think about your answers. Perhaps it is time to change evaluation methods. Your assessment procedures should be designed to give you good information about your employees, translating to greater productivity. Can you go beyond an evaluation tool that simply tells you: "Johnny gets along well with others" year after year? What you really need to know is if: Johnny can give you 15 percent greater productivity, right now, when you need it.

Remember that even a good evaluation system may have holes in it. It might not compensate for personality conflicts, office politics or prejudicial thinking. For example, researchers have found that male bosses are sometimes afraid to evaluate women as honestly as they evaluate men. While the practice makes for polite office culture, hiding constructive feedback that could jumpstart the female employee's career may also be a lost opportunity to jumpstart productivity, company-wide.

Despite such inadequacies, the bottom line for any performance evaluation form is that three basics must be covered: clarify job expectations, review accomplishments, a plan for future performance and development.

Clarifying Expectations

Managers and staffers have a whole host of expectations about their workplace: cooperation, respect, consideration, support, confidence, capability, responsibility, independence, accountability and flexibility. If there is one concept that addresses all of these concerns, it is *communication*. Along with procedural and organizational requirements, political sensitivities and job competence, communication is vital for effective performance on the job, as well as effective evaluations of that performance.

Most of the reasons employees fail to perform well are related to a failure of communication. The following ten reasons are the most common reasons for the lack of productivity, interest or commitment to a job:

1. Employees don't know why they are supposed to do something.

2. They don't know when a task or project begins or ends.

3. They don't know what they're supposed to do.

4. They don't know how to do something.

5. They think they are already doing what was expected.

6. They think your way will not work or their way is better.

7. Something else seems more important.

8. They are not rewarded for doing something—or are not corrected for failing to do it.

9. They are rewarded for *not* doing something—or corrected for not doing it.

10. They think they can't do what you ask.

Clarifying why the employee isn't meeting the expected standards should be a priority. Specifics need to be probed. To do this effectively, the supervisor must be nurturing and constructive with criticism. Subjective judgments on the part of both the supervisor and the employee should be avoided. Each individual must try to offer objective appraisals of his or her actions and expectations.

If you are not the person doing the evaluations, provide good training for your managers to avoid reviews based solely on personal feelings. Be very clear about your expectations for each employment position that has been created in your company. Supply your supervisors with detailed criteria of each position so that they can objectively review your employees.

Armed with that information, your managers can determine first whether or not the employee being reviewed has been given the necessary details of his or her job. You don't want employees who are doing the best they can under the circumstances. Your evaluation process should determine what might be holding your employees back from being the best they can be—and that's all it should do. Managers must be made comfortable with the review process. It should not be a task they dread more than the person being reviewed. Think of your managers as detectives, charged with discovering how your employees can be more productive. If they are then trained to partner with the employee in boosting his or her career, you may dig up the information that is holding the employee (and your productivity) back. Liking or disliking the person they are reviewing should not even be an option for your manager to be successful. A productive review by a manager should be rewarded. Allow them to buy-in to the accomplishments of the employee.

Reviewing Accomplishments

What are the criteria for appraising job responsibilities? They must be representative of the time frame being evaluated. Included should be: core responsibilities, minimum requirements for performing the job, and the goals and objectives of the job. The key is to be specific, detailed and as objective as possible in describing fulfillment of these criteria.

In my experience, a rating system with more than four rating categories is usually inaccurate and inconsistent. According to management guru Douglas McGregor, it is possible to discriminate fairly accurately between outstanding, satisfactory and unsatisfactory performances.

Most supervisors are stuck with an evaluation form they have inherited from their company. It may be confusing with far too many categories, or not enough. It may dwell on evaluating personality traits rather than specific work behavior or on areas not related to the job. If that is the case, it would be beneficial for the supervisor and the employee each to write a detailed summery and attach them to the form. That allows both them both to utilize their own standards in evaluating accomplishments on the job.

Whether you are giving formal or informal feedback, it should be given in a timely fashion. Let the employee know precisely when something happens. Don't wait six months to surprise him or her with the news. It should also be specific and clear. Be it compliment or correction, specifics cover the territory whereas general statements only create a fog. For example, "The course you took in business writing really paid off. The report you turned in last week allowed me to sell our idea to the boss." It helps to be objective as well. Instead of saying the report was outstanding, let the employee know the writing was effective and that it accomplished your shared goal. Identify the specific area of improvement so that he or she can repeat the successful accomplishment. They understand that the new path they are taking is the right one.

Employees want to know exactly what they did that was so right because they want to repeat it. They probably did something new or different that caught your attention, but they may not realize why it pleased you. You do them no favors unless you specifically identify what they did well. Perhaps you have been reluctant to mention something they have been doing wrong because it seems petty to you. Find a way to make this a motivating opportunity. Say something along the lines of "I like this way much better."

Planning for Future Performance and Development

Once the cause of a performance problem is determined, the supervisor and employee should work together to solve it. A developmental attitude toward the employee who needs assistance usually pays off. If a lack of technical know-how is the issue, both the supervisor and the employee should explore further training. If a lack of experience is the problem, and it is felt that the employee is in the right job, it is important to recognize his or her best abilities while offering assurance the company is willing to invest further career development. Expressing confidence through statements such as, "I know you can do it!" will go a long way in nurturing a budding star employee.

Capable and ambitious, Dan was stagnating in a job he hated. His manager, Bob, who was not comfortable with supervisory responsibilities, hated his own job, too. He was passing his negativity on to his subordinates. Although he gave acceptable reviews to the employees under him, his department languished in ineffectiveness and low productivity.

Eventually, Bob left and John replaced him. John picked up on Dan's potential despite his defensive attitude left over from Bob's indifferent administration. John encouraged Dan to begin trying out some of his ideas and stretching his skills. The different management style made a real difference in Dan's performance—and he quickly became the most valuable employee in the department. John had let him out of his mental and emotional constraints by helping him to set and evaluate new goals. Five years later, when John accepted an out-of-town position, Dan was promoted to supervisor. John says Dan's promotion is the kind of success story that makes every manager look good.

The example of John taking some responsibility for Dan's success is a partnership model between manager and employee that companies should be creating. If your managers aren't doing this now, get them the training and incentives to buy into the concept. Strategies that help employees plan for career development contribute to the success of the business and its future. Be it a small business or a large corporation, managers who assist in producing successful growth for employees affect the growth of the business as well. Challenging assignments and moneymaking ideas should be discussed and encouraged at evaluation time. That is one of the most important parts of goal setting. When an employer asks me what can be done to increase productivity, "Where can I start, here and now?" I tell them they can start with this model of managing the career of each and every company employee.

Office manager for a busy dermatologist, Miriam Adams, offers this observation about goal setting: "It does not matter that employees are unable to immediately reach a goal—my greatest satisfaction comes in watching them conquer and grow in their continuing effort to achieve that goal. Employees with no purposeful goal contribute little to office growth or meaning within their own lives. From a management standpoint, if we can be patient while they are striving for this aspiration, we will all be winners."

Supervisors must ask themselves whether they encourage employee's viewpoints for both the company's progress and theirs. Employees will feel valued and search for ways to "win the prize" for themselves and the company. Upper management must consider on-going training and development of supervisors and employees, utilizing in-house services or continuing education They should also offer financial support for these endeavors. The result will be an individual with healthier self-esteem, greater motivation and less need for hand-holding on the part of management.

The Interpersonal Touch

In each segment of an appraisal, especially when dealing with problematic situations, a supervisor's listening skills are her most vital tool. This is also true for the employee. Listening is the link to understanding. Even body language can create a positive or negative influence. Eye contact is essential. Silence and nodding the head can be powerful. Another easy, but effective strategy with active listening is to lean forward when the other person is speaking. Doing so conveys the message that you are listening, interested and ready to respond.

Evaluations usually cover both the positive and negative. To best appraise the situation, likes and dislikes, moods and problems should be put on hold. Spontaneity, especially with praise, gives immediate affirmation. Caution and careful consideration of correction help diffuse the emotional response. When giving criticism, always ask for feedback from the employee. That allows for a repetition of the communication in his or her own words for clarification. It is most effective for the supervisor then, to summarize the discussion for further clarification.

When Evaluations Don't Go Well

If your managers are trained well, unpleasant behavior during the reviews should not be a problem, as long as the criticisms don't come as a complete surprise. Everyone is nervous and uncomfortable in this environment, but negative reviews that have not been previously discussed are unfair and lead to unpleasantness. The employee who is allowed to continue lackluster performance without intervention for several months can be expected to be shocked, hurt and defensive at a negative review.

Strive to show the employee that they can take this negative and turn it into a positive like this: "As you know, I am concerned about your inability to meet deadlines with your projects. I am still trying to figure out how the company can support improvement for you. This review is just clarification for both of us that we are not as successful as we could be in turning this problem around. Have you had any new thoughts on this?"

What if, after the review and subsequent discussions of strengths and weaknesses, the reviewer and employee reach an impasse where matters of improvement are needed? Such a situation cannot be left unresolved, so you may have to involve the human resource department. Rebuttals usually dissipate when a third party joins in the problem solving. It is very important for both supervisor and employee to document the steps taken in working toward the resolution. Both should sign off on the written evaluation, with the employee adding any comments he or she wishes to make.

The Value of Performance Evaluations

The truth about performance evaluations is that they are valuable tools in the process of loving the job you and your employee may hate. Whether you are management or staff, you need feedback to function effectively. Even upper-level executives need feedback.

Performance evaluations are a communication process that should serve as a motivating tool that will enhance productivity. Unmotivated workers who feel management does not care about their development and success spell low productivity and possible failure for a business. Therefore, it is vital both the reviewer and staff person understand the only way to measure productivity, morale and growth on the job is through some type of concrete evaluation process.

Beneficial as the process is, human nature makes both parties uncomfortable with it. It is difficult to sit down with another person and tell him his weaknesses and what he must do to improve. It is also difficult to listen to someone telling you these things. We all have a resistance to being judged. Perhaps that resistance is what also makes supervisors uncomfortable in judging their subordinates. It is understandable. After all, the words you use and the criticism you offer will affect your employees significantly. How they feel about their jobs, and possibly even themselves, can be directly influenced by what you say and how you treat them. Are you aware of the power you have to help make your employees more productive, satisfied workers for your company? Consider your impact carefully. That is not to say you should walk on eggshells and be loath to express criticism or correction. It is crucial, however, that you are aware of how you present the information. When your staff believes you are committed to their development, success and satisfaction on the job, they will find constructive criticism of value. Most importantly, remember to criticize or correct the work behavior, not the person or personality.

If two or more supervisors are involved in the review process, you may discover that you'll encounter more resistance from the employee. This is natural, as it sets up a "two-against-one" scenario for the person being reviewed and they will almost certainly become defensive. In some cases, this may be unavoidable, as one of the other supervisors may be a personnel officer, required to attend.

In order to defuse the situation, you might want to go into the evaluation with your employee as a partner in his or her career. This would change the balance, so it is you and the worker dealing with ("against") the personnel officer. This will make the employee feel there is some kind of advocacy for her or him.

In all performance reviews, express confidence in your employees' efforts. Offer a genuine commitment to helping them achieve goals in the future. Your support—including objective, constructive performance evaluations—will do even more to motivate employees than raises.

Training should be provided for both management and staff to understand the priority of performance evaluations in your business. If you are just placing the evaluation in a folder to forget it, that is fine if everyone—including the employee—knows it. However, if you want your performance review process to be important, it must serve as a tool to motivate your workers to reach their highest potential—and everyone should be aware of the value you place in the process. As one of my colleagues has reminded me, "Although you do not walk on water, a supervisor is expected to get wet trying, every day."

CHAPTER FIFTEEN

MOTIVATING EMPLOYEES TO LOVE THEIR JOBS

Sandra believes the most effective means of motivating her employees is to remind them regularly they could stand to do much better on their jobs, and they have yet to meet her standards of excellence. She thinks creating anxiety in her employees about whether they will still have their jobs by the end of the pay period can't hurt. Her staff responds to her management style by quickly burning out on the job, producing mediocre work, or simply quitting in frustration. Her company's employee turnover is phenomenal.

Bonnie's idea of effective motivation is to remind her employees about past accomplishments, acknowledge present achievements and provide constructive feedback that will improve performance. She offers tangible and intangible rewards on a consistent basis. The results are Bonnie's employees are interested in their work, willing and able to meet their shared goals with the company and remain with the company as dedicated loyal workers.

Who would you say has mastered the art of motivation?

Basically, there are two motivators for human beings, and one or the other of these is behind every behavior known to humans. They are fear and desire.

Fear, of course, is the negative motivator. It is the one that Sandra uses. When an employer activates an employee's fears, the result is the employee's avoidance of something he perceives as harmful or painful—in this case, the work he is supposed to do. Although fear can be a valid and necessary motivator (in avoiding poisonous snakes, for instance), an employer needs to look at how fear causes destructive behavior in the work environment. This can manifest itself in such things as starting rumors or sabotaging each other's work. Fear motivation actually stifles productivity. Employees begin to spend work hours thinking of ways to assure their job by making others look bad. That's true especially if they haven't been given the necessary tools to produce more and do their job better.

Desire, used by managers like Bonnie, is a positive motivator that can lead to achievement, success and job satisfaction. Of course, it can have its negative consequences, if the desire is a wrong or unrealistic one. However, you will find that desire is a much more effective motivator for almost any goal. Employees need to work toward goals they know can be achieved. Has your desired outcome ever been demonstrated? Do your employees know that it can be done, given their skills and experience? Your workers need to know that the productivity goals you set for them are do-able. They need to have a model of how to achieve them, if it is greater than what they have done in the past. Show your employees that you believe in them and support their success with your company.

Desiring the rewards of success is far more stimulating than fearing the consequences of personal failure. A worker who fears failure, in terms of your firing them, certainly won't care if your business fails—that's the problematic result for you. Numerous psychological studies prove animals and humans are motivated to better results by rewards rather than fear of punishment. Positive motivation is more conducive to reaching a goal or learning a new behavior. It is vital that managers know that they can better motivate their employees to greater success and achievement with the promise of tangible or intangible (praise and appreciation) rewards than with the threat of punishment.

Be the Kind of Leader *You* Would Follow

For a leader whose goal is to "get people to do things," it is important to start with a positive self-image. After all, how can you bring out the best in others if you aren't motivated by the best in yourself? Here is a list of the ten qualities as being essential to a leader based on those first set forth by Joseph Jaworski, chairman of the American Leadership Forum. Give yourself a brief evaluation as you review it.

- Mastery of self: Be in control of your emotions. Get in top physical condition.

- Empathy: Understand people and their concerns.

- Wholeness of purpose: Know what results you want and do what is possible to make them happen. Be positive and proactive, not reactive.

- <u>Self-confidence</u>: You must be able to act despite doubts.

- <u>Authenticity and congruence</u>: What you say and what you do must match up to assure personal credibility.

- <u>Ability to communicate</u>: Communication is essential to motivate and build morale.

- <u>Ability to mediate</u>: You must combine activities and build coalitions.

- <u>Integrity</u>: Develop mature ethical values.

- <u>Intelligence</u>: If you do not know something, know how to get information and use it.

- <u>Energy</u>: Have the drive and stamina to stay on top.

These ten characteristics will render you fully capable of developing the skill to motivate others. Identify your weak areas—nobody is perfect! Find those of your managers who are strong in your weak characteristics to help you balance your organization. Hire a personnel director to teach your managers the skills they need to motivate your workers and increase your productivity and efficiency. Building a team of motivated managers and workers can give your business all it needs to be successful in any economy.

To assist your management team in the fine art of motivation, here are some guidelines to follow, captured by the acronym <u>MOTIVATE</u>:

Maximize employee potential

Offer opportunities for growth

Trust employees to do their jobs

Involve employees in company decisions

Value employee differences

Allow for mistakes

Throw away threats, punishment and fear

Encourage through praise and rewards

Maximize Employee Potential, or "Potentialize"

When employees feel their skills have been evaluated and applied in the most effective manner for the position they are in, they feel more secure about stretching themselves. By placing small challenges along the way, employers will inspire their workers to discover and use their abilities. On the same note, giving employees the tools to do their jobs (i.e., up-to-date computers, informational seminars, clerical assistance and so on) will also help them reach their fullest potential.

Offer Opportunities for Growth. Employees need goals to grow. They should actively participate in the goal-setting process—both their own and the company's. Sit down with employees and pinpoint the company's goals, especially those that include them. Listen carefully as they outline the attainments they have set for themselves—after all, they know themselves better than anyone else. Awareness that they have your support to reach the goals they have set is a surefire motivator.

Trust Employees to Do Their Jobs. Hovering—it is death to motivation. Give employees the responsibility for doing their job—then leave them alone to do it! Motivation is highest in organizations that encourage openness and trust. Let employees assume more responsible tasks, and productivity will take off. Once an assignment is delegated to an employee and you have left him alone to do the job, he will feel valued and respected. If you continue to check up on him or her, you are sending a clear message they can't be trusted. Delegating with trust can be empowering—and a powerful motivator.

Involve Employees in Company Decisions. Not every company decision can—or even should—involve employees, but many can. An important research finding in motivational psychology is that people who have no control over their lives become passive. They view the direction of their lives as external to themselves. By bringing employees into the decision loop, you not only tap into your most valuable resource, you let them know you respect their input. Making them aware of decisions that affect them is a way to contribute to their successful development.

Value Employee Differences. As we have seen throughout this book, different people have diverse needs based on their personality types, work styles, lifestyles and more. Recognizing those differences is crucial to effective motivation. After all, what satisfies one person may not satisfy another.

The observant manager will determine what meets the needs of employee A and employee Z, then act accordingly. For instance, an employee who is a people-person should be given the opportunity to work with others. Command-person employees would most likely enjoy more task-oriented activities, and so on. By the same token, some people require closer supervision than others. In order to optimize performance and individual motivation, an evaluation of the supervisory needs of the employee can determine how much participation is required of you.

Allow for Mistakes. It's going to happen: a mistake will occur, or a level of performance will not be quite up to par. That requires the delicate art of constructive criticism. You want to refrain from behavior, words or action that inhibits motivation or growth. To bring about improvement, wisdom is required when giving feedback. If the employee knows that you are criticizing with the intention of helping him or her improve performance, they will not be as defensive as they might be. It is also important to remember that you should focus on the behavior, not the person. If the value of the person is under attack, the criticism becomes demoralizing and that could interfere with your goals of productivity.

Save your comments for a private meeting, limiting the feedback to one problem. Offer assistance, provide suggestions on how the employee might improve his performance at the task, and state your confidence in his ability to correct or change the situation as necessary. Remember, too, that knowing a person may make a mistake yet still be a valuable employee, goes a long way toward positive motivation. Ask if there is something going on in his or her life that may have distracted them, and offer support to deal with the distraction. Employees need to know they are not just numbers in a cubicle. When they feel valued, they can forgive themselves for the mistake and continue working with healthy self-esteem and loyalty toward the company's goals. Gratitude helps the employee prevent further mistakes because they are invested in success.

Throw Away Threats, Punishments and Fear. Threatening termination is not the most positive way to motivate employees. In fact, threats and punishments create that negative motivator we discussed earlier: fear. Avoidance behavior can become the norm with this approach, and it also encourages unpredictable and imprecise behavior.

Fear is damaging, because it sets up constant worry, which distracts your employee's concentration and sets them up for burnout. Your employees concentrate on keeping their jobs at all cost, instead of being productive and efficient. They just won't care. Worry over losing their job because they don't measure up ends up becoming a self-fulfilling prophecy for the threatened employee.

Encourage through Praise and Rewards. It can be something as simple as a handwritten note on your letterhead or a brief call during the day. Avoid the "no news is good news" method of approving employee performance. Recognition for a job well done is without a doubt one of the most essential motivators there is. People need to feel important. Remind them the job they do counts in the grand scheme of things—and of course it does, or you would never have felt the need to fill that job position. Tell employees you need them in order to be successful, and they will do everything they can to prove you right and show your faith in them is well placed.

Bonuses and other more tangible rewards also serve as powerful motivators. In fact, a growing number of businesses are offering workers extra financial rewards for meeting results-oriented goals. From employee profit sharing plans to quarterly awards for greater profit than the company budgeted in a period of time, bonuses are attractive for everyone.

Employers are fearful of across-the-board raises in this poor economy. It's great to give raises when business is doing well, but when production slows or business begins a precarious slide, employers may have to cut positions or salaries to balance the budget. These are demoralizing measures for the workforce and for your business. By offering a positive reward for hard work and success, using a formula that protects the company's bottom line, workers feel safe in the slow times and successful members of a winning team when times are good. They will continue to contribute their best efforts, while trying to reach shared goals.

One reward that is becoming more popular for companies is giving a new benefit that comes with minimal cost and has a built-in, personalized, self-esteem booster. It is my first suggestion for employers who ask how they can reward employees with another paid holiday, without shutting down their business and slowing productivity. Think about giving your employees their birthday off with pay. It is unlikely that you will have several employees taking the same day off. Another reward is to give your employees a "floating holiday." This is an excellent idea for acknowledging your diverse workforce and earns respect from your clients who are just as different. Ethnic and religious groups have different days that mean something special to them, and are celebrated with family members gathering from far away. This choice could keep your business open when your competitors are closed.

Keep in mind that rewards should always be deserved, or they lose their impact for reinforcement and motivation. You also need to make sure you are rewarding the right person for increased productivity and profitability. By avoiding some kind of company-wide bonus formula and picking out one or two stars to reward, you could be setting yourself up for failure.

I know of a company that rewarded the person who sold the most car parts in an auto repair shop. The company repaired cars, and is not an auto parts store, *per se*, but management created a position for an Auto Parts Salesperson to inventory, stock and order car parts. During a monthly meeting, when the praise for the parts person started once again, a young mechanic stood up and asked, "Does anyone realize that we rarely sell auto parts around here? It's the mechanics in the shop who get the parts to repair the cars. We sell the merchandise. The parts salesman just pulls the parts we need from the shelf."

If you aren't sure what is creating your increased productivity, hold the praise and rewards until you investigate. This is also when a boss recognizes that team building better serves the company. Using rewards to pit employees against one another is just plain bad business; it is not positive motivation.

Other Ways to Boost Motivation

Make sure employees understand your expectations. Don't allow misunderstanding about what you expect from an employee and what the employee thinks you expect to cause confusion and frustration.

Remove barriers to achievement. A pebble in one person's road to progress may be a boulder in someone else's. Seek to recognize and remove any obstacles that may be discouraging an employee in his or her attempts to do a better job.

Be a listener. When employees have a complaint, take time to understand what they are saying. Productivity is hindered when even minor problems surface, and they can become blown out of proportion. It also contributes to an employee's feelings of worth to find that his or her concerns are of some significance to you.

Note improvements, large and small. This is especially important if you assigned an employee a new task. Consistent reinforcement is vital in order to encourage progress in the early stages of performance.

Inspire by example. Show your employees how motivated you are through your behavior and attitude. If they see you plodding through the halls with a frown on your face and a grumble on your lips, they may copy your performance. Or worse, worry that something is wrong with the company. That is how fear and rumors begin.

Keeping the Motivator Motivated

How do you manage your own motivation? Do you even think about it? It is difficult for your workers to be enthusiastic about their productivity when they perceive doubt in their leader. It's that simple.

Giving praise, encouraging and motivating others will, in and of itself, provide you with motivation. There is nothing like the hum of productivity and the smiles of satisfied employees to help you love the job you have. But there are a few other suggestions to help you stay fresh and motivated, especially in an economy that will distract you.

Set your own goals. Where do you want to be on your job in the next few months or years? Take time to jot down those goals in a small journal. Read them periodically to help keep you motivated and focused.

Stay informed. A wealth of information is available through seminars, cassettes, CDs, books and professional magazines. Keep on top of your field by grabbing a few moments at lunch to head to your local library and do a little research. You can appoint an employee to give you updates and reports in targeted areas. Sign up for a class that is work-related or enroll in a course that allows you to explore a subject that has always interested you.

Sweep away negative cobwebs from your thoughts. Having hassles on the job, car troubles, the post-holiday blahs? Sometimes your mind can become cluttered with life's little annoyances. They seep into the job before you know it and prohibit you from being the motivator you are. Clear your mind by quiet meditation, reading the Bible or other inspirational books. Take time to help a community organization or simply enjoy a stroll in a park for a mind-clearing, energy boost.

I am a firm believer in taking the time to change gears. If you live fairly close to your job and have a lively family at home, don't rush between one stressful situation to another. Take a time-out in between work and family to change gears and mentally clear your mind. Life is too short to spend your days in one anxiety-filled environment after another. Just like you learned to push in the clutch when you started driving a standard-shift car, give yourself a buffer between one job and the next, or your brain will grind, like the gears in that car. Stop at the gym or better yet, walk home and stop by the local fire station or drug store to get your blood pressure checked. You can be just as proactive in your life as you are in business management.

Associate with positive people. Stay motivated by being around other motivators. Let yourself be inspired by fellow successful managers. Share your concerns, stimulate your thinking and allow others to help your enlarge your capacity to enjoy the work you do.

Occasionally, I meet seminar attendees who tell me they won't get anything from my "How to Love the Job You Hate" seminars. These people say they already enjoy a consistently high level of job satisfaction—and they always give credit to their managers. One said, "My supervisor has so much faith in my potential that even when I have doubts about my abilities, I just can't let him down. I keep working and before I know it, the project is done and I'm on to the next assignment. That's why I love my job and I can't imagine working for anyone else." Would that all businesses have managers like that!

CHAPTER SIXTEEN

THE WHEEL OF LIFE: BALANCE IN AN

UNBALANCED WORLD

What do you want out of life? How will loving your job benefit your emotional needs and help you achieve your goals? If you don't like your job, you already know that it has affected your emotions, your physical well-being and your personal life. It has made you feel out of balance. People need to feel a sense of wholeness to know that their lives have made a difference and have a purpose.

Benjamin Franklin was a statesman, an inventor and a publisher. He wrote and planned the script for his life and he acted it out. His life was a work of art—and Franklin himself was the artist. By sharing how he lived, he illustrated that there is more to life than simply reacting to it—that in fact, one can take a hand in shaping or influencing the events.

As you read this final chapter and you are an employer or employee, worker or supervisor, pay attention to where you are in your life today and where you want to be tomorrow. Life is too complex a process to say that all, or even some of it, can be planned. It is a matter of degree. But if you choose to have a balanced life, it will be one that is rich in variety and choice. Like Benjamin Franklin, you can write the script for your life and see the future unfold.

The Wheel of Life: How the Spokes Support the Rim

One year I got a new bike for Christmas. It was the prettiest bike I had ever seen. My friend Sandy and I went riding, and I felt proud to be on my new bike. The ride was so smooth—as if I was flying. All of a sudden Sandy got too close and her bike pedal got stuck in my front wheel. Five spokes were pulled out. After the accident I noticed that the wheel gave me a rough ride and that smooth feeling was gone.

That's the way the wheel of life is. If one of the spokes is weak or missing, the ride is more difficult and uncomfortable. It takes a conscious effort to devote equal time to each area of your life. If you are unable to devote equal time, your life gets out of balance, which can result in confusion and chaos.

Let's consider the six primary areas that influence our lives:

Financial / Career

It is ironic to me that people spend the greatest amount of waking hours with people we don't know anything about. Our co-workers are people we don't get to choose to be with. What is left of our time, energy, passion, and concentration belongs to those who matter most to us. Your job is necessary to support those we love and to provide for them. That is why the financial spoke in the "wheel of life" becomes so large and out of balance with the rest of the wheel.

In most cases, we have little control over the hours we spend working and commuting. If this is so for you, try to plan your activities with your own wheel of life in mind. Focus on the areas of your life where you do have some control and flexibility. Remember that your job is important but that it is not everything. Don't let your job overshadow your time with your spouse and children. Don't let your career rob you of your health and spirituality. When you look at the financial spoke in your wheel, find out how well it is balanced with the rest of your wheel. How would loving your job benefit your emotional needs and help you to achieve your goals? Surveys reveal that the most highly valued aspects of a job are related to basic fundamental needs—over and above any monetary rewards. It is your duty to yourself to determine what you need from a job. Ask yourself these questions to find the balance for your wheel of life:

- Does your job give you a sense of purpose?
- Do you feel you are accomplishing something in your life?
- Do you feel your life has an effect on the world?
- Does your job give you a sense of belonging—being part of something?
- Does your job give you the opportunity to be recognized and ap-

preciated for who you are and the talents you bring to it?

- Does your job maximize your full potential?

- Do you earn less than you could make in your job, but know that this job offers a better balance in your "wheel of life." For example, is your job close enough to your home, that you feel good about sacrificing money for more time with your family?

If you are trying to sell yourself on your current job, you need to decide how you will answer those questions. Your answers will have a tremendous impact on your personal motivation. You can be motivated, fulfilled, successful and profitable in your job. Don't give up on yourself or on your job yet. Believe that the possibilities are there, and you can even affect the bottom line for your company in a positive way.

Personal

How do you get to know yourself? Most people are so busy that they don't take time out for themselves. I often ask my seminar attendees, "How did you end up in that job or that marriage?" Many reply, "I don't know—but thirty years later, here I am."

Have you ever had a problem and for the life of you, you couldn't come up with the answer? Finally, you went to sleep and at three o'clock in the morning you woke up with a solution. That's no accident. You got quiet and the answer emerged.

Consider these ideas for a happier, healthier mental attitude:
- Be flexible.

- Tolerate frustration and uncertainty.

- Do not defensive about your past, overwhelmed by the present or fearful of the future.

- Be open-minded and non-judgmental.

- Be willing to learn from others.

- Challenge traditional ways of doing things.

- Make decisions without being overly-influenced by others.

- Be sensitive and empathetic. Be aware of other people's thoughts, feelings and needs

Listen to yourself. The first way to get in touch with that personal part of you is by listening to the voice within. You might have to make an appointment to have quiet time with yourself. If someone wants to interrupt, tell them you are already busy at that time. Make sure you keep that appointment.

Keep a journal. The second way to get in touch with that personal part of you is by keeping a journal. That is not to be confused with keeping a diary. A journal is a personal recording of your thoughts, feelings, ideas and dreams. It is not just a recording of who and what you see each day.

Several years ago, my life took a turn for the worse when I lost four loved ones almost simultaneously. I had been teaching about the power of writing one's feelings in a journal. Now I had unbearable grief and I didn't know what to do with it. I pulled out my pen and began to write. I wrote for hours; I wrote until I was exhausted and able to sleep. Something miraculous and healing happened as I transferred the feelings from my heart to the yellow legal pad. I began to feel relief, and as the months passed, I could see just how far I had come. I only had to look at the writing I had done months before to see what I had overcome. Richard Bach in his book *Illusions* tells us that sometimes the teacher needs the lesson himself. I'm grateful that I was given the opportunity to learn what I had been teaching.

I cannot say enough about the healing attributes of keeping a journal. Somehow, I was able to transfer all those feelings of grief out of me and onto the paper. As Benjamin Franklin so aptly put it, there is great satisfaction in self-examination, especially when one is able to overcome many of life's challenges.

Find your joy. The third way you get in touch with that personal part of you is by identifying what gives you joy and making time for it. For the next few moments, think of some of the things that bring you joy. Make a list of ten things that you do for fun. Next to that list, write the last time you did those things. Now ask yourself whether or not you would have done those things ten years ago. Are there things on your fun list that you can't remember when you last did them? You may also still be doing the exact same things today that you did ten years ago. That's not all bad, but the point is that you may not be allowing new people, opportunities and challenges into your life. Maybe you are just stuck in the same old rut. Have you changed your appetites, and are you open to all the best life has to offer?

Take steps toward achieving your goals. Goals are a statement of faith. They motivate you to reach new levels of maturity in every area of your life. In several of the seminars I teach, the attendees spend at least an hour writing out their spiritual, family, vocational and social goals. The goals must be measurable, realistic and obtainable. You should have checkpoints for measuring your progress. If you have ever gone on a diet, you know that you have a desired target weight and that you get on the scale periodically get on a scale to measure your progress.

The first step in setting your goals is to evaluate your present situation; determine where you are at the moment. Now decide where you choose to go and how you will get there. It will give you a sense of direction and purpose. Try to reduce the goals you choose to work on to a vital few, because you will need the time, energy or money to carry out the plan for achieving them.

Goal setting is a continual process, and it calls for a strong sense of priority and self-confidence. Start out with easy, short-term goals that you know you can meet fairly quickly, to get you started with the satisfaction of winning. Another way to approach this is to decide on things you want to attain in two or five year. From there work backwards to the present setting smaller, short-term goals that will set you up to succeed.

You can achieve anything you want if you want it badly enough and can imagine yourself being there when you reach your goal. Imagine what everything around you will look like to make your dream as vivid and specific as possible. I still believe this, but as I tell my seminar attendees, becoming a brain surgeon takes a bit longer time than, say, learning to make a good soufflé.

Here are some steps to follow as you set goals:

- Decide what is really important to you. Eliminate irrelevant half-hearted desires.

- Set priorities and write each item out in order of importance. Grade them (A, B, C, etc.). Your most important goals are As and Bs. Cs carry a lower priority.

- Every day, write down the tasks that will help you achieve high priority goals. Also include the desired date of the accomplishment of each goal.

- Do it now. Don't procrastinate. Reread your list at least three times a day and take action.

- Develop your action plan. What is the first thing you will do toward accomplishing your goal? When will you begin?

- Visualize yourself as already having accomplished your goal. Allow your mind to work for you and continue to have faith and patience. It will happen.

- Avoid distractions. Say no to interruptions and requests that clearly have nothing to do with your goals.

- When you want something, act as if you already have it or have accomplished it. That will help you stay on your path of success. When you think and act confidently you will begin to feel, then actually become confident and successful.

Remember that goal setting is critical for your personal and professional success, but that *it is done by imperfect people in an imperfect world.* What seems important today may not be in five years. That's all right. Nothing you have done is wasted. Your goals will help you reach your potential to be more of who you already are. They will recharge your batteries and keep you interested in this complicated thing called life.

Mentors. Can you remember a teacher who was a major influence on your life? If you want another way to get in touch with that personal part of you, then find a person whom you respect and who will take the time to help you grow.

I have had a series of mentors in my life. When I was in high school, I had a counselor who said I would never make it at a big college like Ohio State. Fortunately, I had a wonderful English teacher, Ron Price, who believed in me. I couldn't wait to go to his English class. Students, who hated English, loved his English class.

I went to Ohio State, was accepted into the honor's college, and graduated with a 4.0 and a Master's degree. At Ohio State, I had another mentor. In order to complete my education, I had to take a speech class. Public speaking was one of my biggest nightmares. They say the number one fear, especially for successful people, is the fear of speaking in public. It holds back so many students, from middle school on up through college, and some people manage to become very successful, but still get weak in the knees when they are asked to speak in public, or in front of others. Because of a caring professor who sensed my fear and empathized with it, I was able to overcome my speaking anxiety, and I now make my living as a professional speaker. I've often wondered what career choice I would have made without her positive influence.

Less than ten years after graduating from Ohio State, I acquired another mentor. I met Zig Ziglar at a National Speaker's Association convention. I wonder if he knows, today, what an impact he made on my life. I followed him to Dallas, Texas, where I attended his "Born to Win" seminar. It was more than an educational experience; it was a life-changing event. I had a spiritual awakening and have never been the same, since. I listened to his advice, as have thousands of other people across the country. Mr. Ziglar has been a source of continual inspiration for me, and I will always be grateful for his encouraging words.

Find a mentor—and after you've grown—be a mentor. When you give of yourself, you get back a thousand-fold.

Social

The social part of the wheel has to do with your social conscience. What are you willing to give back to society, expecting nothing in return? Are you associated with a cause or group? Are you involved with your church, synagogue or temple, or supporting a political or human rights agenda? Have you taken time out of your busy schedule to help someone less fortunate than you? It's easy to feel sorry for yourself in today's crazy world. There is never enough time and always too much to do. But one way to get off the subject of you is to find someone who is less fortunate than you are and help him. If you don't feel grateful for what you have, find someone who has less—you'll be cured, right away.

Physical

Ralph Waldo Emerson said that your health is your wealth. My friend's mom says, "If you don't have your health, you don't have nothin'." Your physical well-being is an important part of you. How healthy are you? When was the last time you had a check-up? You can learn to be pro-active. A routine check-up can identify high blood pressure, which can lead to stroke. Cancer can be detected in its early stages when it is most easily treated, and many other diseases and conditions can be avoided or more easily cured.

The body can take a lot of punishment and still keep functioning. Most health care professionals believe that disease is caused by a reckless lifestyle or distorted outlook. Jobs that place high demands on workers and give little autonomy or appreciation are stress producing. The result is negativity and health challenges.

You know what you should be doing to stay healthy. We all do. If you need a little push in the right direction, think of your family, loved ones and those whose careers depend upon you. What would happen to them if you weren't there?

You need to enjoy your work. Take care of your personal growth. Develop intimate relationships. Rest, exercise and play. You need to pay attention to what you eat and be sure to laugh a lot. Laughing leads to greater respiratory activity, cardiovascular stimulation, and increased endorphin production. Smiling makes you feel better and look younger.

There are some basic ingredients to being healthy:

- Take care of yourself. Understand that your physical health affects every area of your life.

- Listen to what your body is telling you. If you feel unusually fatigued or "off," discover why.

- Illness and disease can be a message to take a new road in your life.

Your health is the most valuable possession you have. Some people are enriched because of good health and others are impoverished by bad health. It is our well-being, our essence. Remember to treat your physical body with respect. You deserve it!

Emotional

The emotional part of the wheel has to do with your relationship to your family, friends and colleagues. Take a few moments to answer the following questions:

- Who are the ten most important people in your life?

- When was the last time you told them how valuable they are to you?

- Have you ever told one of those people, "You are special," in part, because of what he means to you?

- When was the last time you looked in the mirror and said, "I love myself," "I am unique," or "I am special"?

I once gave a seminar in Ohio to a group of insurance executives. They were mostly men in the audience that day and I asked them those four questions. When I stepped down from the podium, the president of the association took the microphone. He told them that several years earlier he had tried to tell his parents how he felt about them. His mother seemed awkward, brushing the moment away by telling her son that it wasn't necessary to say the obvious; they knew how he felt. But John said he couldn't remember ever telling them how much he loved them and how grateful he was for the sacrifices they made as parents. With tears in his eyes, John went on to explain that it wasn't more than a few weeks later that he lost both of his parents; they were killed by a drunk driver. He urged his colleagues to tell their families and friends what they felt today, before it was too late.

As I lecture around the country, I am constantly reminded of that story. I make it a point to encourage others to say the words of love and gratitude that dwell in their hearts. It makes no sense to live with regret. It is the lost moments in life that hurt us and hold us back.

Spiritual

Dr. Rene Rust, an author, former Catholic nun and friend with whom I've done many seminars, defines spirituality as believing in something outside of yourself. Some people call this outside influence their Higher Power, their Creator or God.

If you want to grow in the spiritual area of your life, it is important to have fellowship with people of like values and to pray or meditate on a regular basis. It is hard to hear what God has to say, if you don't take time to listen.

When your spiritual spoke is strong, you know you are not traveling through life alone. I can remember when I thought I had to handle everything by myself. What a burden I carried! It is refreshing to know God is there during those dark moments in our lives when we cannot see an end to our sorrow. God is there with me in sadness and joy, and through my spiritual relationship with God, I feel my every step is guarded against trouble.

When you have a relationship with God, you will not face the trials and tribulations of life alone. Sunshine lies ahead, beyond the darkness. But many people lack confidence in God. They stay depressed and uncertain. People who lack confidence in God are like people who will not drive a car up a hill because they cannot be sure there is a road beyond the top of the hill. They have no faith.

On his first voyage to the New World, Christopher Columbus sailed for sixty-nine days through unknown waters, with a rebellious crew, struggling against terrible storms. One day's entry in his ship's log bears these five words alone: "This day we sailed on." There was no other land in sight, no identifiable latitude or longitude to record, no odometer to tell him how many miles he had come, and no map to tell him how far he had to go. Sometimes in life, you don't know where you are or where you are going, but you know you have to go on. Pull out a piece of paper and write, "This day I sailed on," or, "This day I kept on going."

A Final Word

I have covered a lot of territory in this book, and I don't pretend to have all the answers you need. But, if you'll try to put some of these ideas into action, you'll discover a definite change in your situation. Power is the extent to which you can link your capacity for action with your inner capacity for reflection. In other words, how much of your mental and emotional insight can you put into action? If you've learned anything from this book, will you act on it?

While you reflect on changing the way you feel about your job, think about the following questions:

- Do you look forward to starting your day?

- When you are handed a challenging assignment, do you dive into it with confidence?

- Do you speak up, set limits and say no when necessary?

- Do you readily admit your own mistakes?

- Do you refuse to allow someone else's bad mood or difficult behavior to affect your feelings about your job?

- Do you think for yourself in spite of your boss or co-workers?

- Do you feel safe being honest in your working relationships?

- Does hard work exhilarate your?

- Is your job satisfaction measured in other than monetary ways?

- Do you walk with your head up, your back straight, look people in the eye and inspire confidence?

When you can answer yes to those questions, you know you are in a job you love. Loving your job starts with loving yourself. If you love your job, tell your employer, supervisor or co-workers. Give others the gift of knowing they have succeeded in creating the work environment that will be most productive. Let someone else know you can reach your full potential in this job, because of his or her management style. Tell her you feel valued and appreciated. We all must learn to celebrate the positive areas of life, at least as much as we complain over the negative ones. Using gratitude and praise, workers have the power to change the way businesses manage by being as productive as they can in healthy and supportive places of work.

Put these ideas into action. They have been discovered by countless others who believe loving their life's work is vital to their mental health and physical well-being—their very purpose on this earth. My sincere hope is you will experience the joy in your job, and in your life, you deserve. After all, teaching you and others to *Love the Job You Hate,* is my life's work. Your success is my success.

SUGGESTED READING

The 7 Habits of Highly Effective People by Stephen Covey, 1990, Simon & Schuster, New York.

The 100 Simple Secrets of Successful People: What Scientists Have Learned and How You Can Use It by David Niven, Ph.D., 2002, Harper San Francisco.

Coping with Difficult People by Robert M. Bramson, Ph.D, 1988, Dell / Random House, New York.

Emotional Intelligence by Daniel Goleman, 1995 Bantam Books, New York

Excuse Me, Your Life is Waiting: The Astonishing Power of Feelings by Lynn Grabhorn, 2000, Hampton Roads Publishing, Charlottesville, VA.

The Four Temperaments: A Rediscovery of the Ancient Way of Understanding Health and Character by Randy Rolfe, 2002, Marlowe & Co., New York.

Full Steam Ahead! Unleash the Power of Vision in Your Company and Your Life by Kenneth Blanchard and Jesse Stoner 2003, Berrett-Koehler Pub., San Francisco.

Also by Blanchard: *Gung Ho! Turn On the People in Any Organization,* 1997, William Morrow, New York.

I Don't Know What I Want, But I Know It's Not This: A Step-By-Step Guide to Finding Gratifying Work by Julie Jansen, 2003, Penguin USA, New York.

Life Strategies: Doing What Works, Doing What Matters by Phillip McGraw, Ph.D. 1999, Hyperion, New York.

Monster Lies: A Woman's Guide to Controlling Her Destiny by Sally Franz and Jennifer Webb, 2002, Beagle Bay Books, Reno, NV.

Now, Discover Your Strengths by Marcus Buckingham and Donald. O. Clifton, 2002, Free Press, New York.

Please Understand Me II: Temperament, Character, Intelligence by David Keirsey, 1998, Prometheus Nemesis Book Co., Del Mar, CA.

Self-Esteem: A Proven Program of Cognitive Techniques for Assessing, Improving, and Maintaining Your Self-Esteem 3rd Edition, by Matthew McKay, Ph.D. and Patrick Fanning, 2000, New Harbinger Publications, Oakland, CA.

Top Performance by Zig Ziglar, 2003, Fleming H. Revell, Grand Rapids, MI.

ABOUT THE AUTHOR

Business consultant Jane Boucher received her Bachelor of Science and Master of Science from Ohio State University. She has done doctoral work at the University of South Florida and has been an adjunct professor at the University of Dayton, Wright State University and Sinclair Community College.

Ms. Boucher has authored three previous books, *The Assertive Communication Workbook* (Career Track), *The Body-Mind Connection*, the original *How to Love the Job You Hate* (Thomas Nelson, Co. Publishers) that also became an audio book (Padgett-Thompson). She has contributed to: *Ordinary Women...Extraordinary Success: Everything You Need to Excel, from America's Top Women Motivators* (Career Press), *Star Spangled Speakers* (Royal Books) and the audio book *Sound Selling . . . Do's Don'ts for Boosting Self Esteem* (Nightingale Conant).

She is also a nationally syndicated newspaper columnist appearing in business journals such as the *Dayton Ohio Business Journal* and the Santa Rosa, California *North Bay Business Journal*. She is a regular contributor to the "Voices" column for *The Northern Nevada Business Weekly,* her observations have appeared in and Nevada's premier community newspaper *The Sierra Sage.* Other articles in publications such as *Menu & More Magazine* in the "Lifestyles and More" column.

She worked with chemically dependant young people before going into her professional speaking career. Ms. Boucher has earned a Certified Speaking Professional (CSP) designation, a distinction awarded to less than 8 percent of all professional speakers.

Today she owns Boucher Consultants, a nationally recognized firm specializing in organizational effectiveness, professional growth and communications. She is a high-energy speaker and executive coach with clients ranging from small business to *Fortune 500* companies such as: General Motors, IBM, *Inc. Magazine* and the United States Air Force. She has received praise from such

185

notables as Senator Orrin Hatch and has shared a podium with General Norman Schwartzkopf.

Ms. Boucher is currently at work on *Surviving Him: How to Stay Out Once You Get Out*, a book about spouse abuse.

For more information about Ms. Boucher's company or to ask her questions, please go to www.janeboucher.org.

Index

A

Absenteeism 142
Abuse
  domestic violence 145–147
  on-the-job 105, 108
Adams, Miriam 160
Addiction 143–144
Americans with Disabilities Act 143, 146
American Leadership Forum. *See* Jaworski, Joseph
Anger 103–108
  careless vocalization 105, 107
  confrontation 106
  deflecting 105
  expressing 104
  listening skills 105–106
  on-the-job abuse 105, 108
  petty annoyances 106
Attention Deficit Disorder (ADD) 136
Attitude 9, 95, 153, 170

B

Bach, Richard
  Illusions 175
Behavioral Disabilities. *See* Disabilities
Behavior Anchored Rating Scales (BARS) 154
Bilingual 149
Body Language 50–51, 160
Bosses 15, 36
  communication 38, 42–44
  empathy and understanding 43
  empowerment 41
  feedback 41–43
  good management 38
  managing your boss 42–44
  personality type 44–47
  supportive 39
Burn-out 93
Burnett, Carol 72
Burns, George 8
Bush, George W. 27, 30

C

Career Planning 41
Cleese, John 96
Clinton, Bill 27, 30
Co-workers 13
  acceptance 56
  body language 50–51
  communication 49
  conflicts 48
  empathy 54
  forgive 55
  humor 53
  listening skills 50–51
  personality type 52–53
  personal responsibility 51
  praise 53
  respect 51
  support 56
  team 56
  trust 56
Communication 156–158, 161–163

Index

Community service 19
  adopt a class 19
  cooperative educational effort 20
  fund-raising events 19
  Habitat for Humanity 19
  holiday party 19
  internships 20
  life skills 19
  volunteer 20
Companies 58
  adapt yourself to 65
  compromise 65
  culture 58, 63–67
  destructive cultural patterns 65
  downsizing 59
  ethics 67–69
  mission statement 68
  "new" position 60
  office politics 63–64
  organizational chart 59
  personality type 64
  size 59
  values 69
  where your job fits in 59
  workaholics 65
Complaining 12
Creative Break 10
Critical Incidents Log 155
Criticism 13, 79, 99
  anger 103
  constructive 99, 101
  listening skills 102–103
  negative 100
  personality type 102
  responsibility for failures 102
  self-esteem 101
  timing 101
Cross-training 12
Culture, Corporate 58–67
  destructive patterns 65

D

Delegate 12
Depression 93–94, 122, 142–145
Disabilities

  behavioral 135–136
  physical 146
Domestic Violence 145–147
Downsizing 59
Drug and Alcohol Addiction 144

E

Einstein, Albert 28, 30
Emerson, Ralph Waldo 178
Employees
  apprenticeship program 150
  bilingual 149
  difficulties with 133–140
  education 149
  Employee Handbook 139
  generation gap 134, 135
  incorrigible 138
  motivating 163–171
  personality type 136–137
  Policies and Procedures manual 139
  problem, handling 139–140
  Standard Operating Procedures (SOP)
    139
  team-building 147–148
  team mentors 150
Employee Handbook 65, 122
Employee Problems 141
  addiction 143–144
  Attention Deficit Disorder (ADD) 136
  behavioral disabilities 135
  depression 142–143
  domestic violence 144–146
  employee surveys 149
  literacy 147
  mental illIness 142
  physically challenged 146
  self-esteem 144
  stress 141–142
  support programs 151
  workaholics 65
Empowerment 41, 147, 154
Entrepreneurs 60–63, 117
Ethics 66–68
Exercise 11

F

Fear 150, 163–164, 167
Federal Job Training Partnership Act
    (JTPA) 150
Feedback 41–43, 139, 158
Fool's Rule 96
Franklin, Benjamin 172, 175
Fund-raising Events 19

G

General Electric (GE) 36, 38
Generation Gap 134–135
  older supervisor 134
  younger supervisor 134
Getting Fired / Laid-off 121, 121–130
  balance personal life and work 122
  career change 127
  depression 122
  grief 122
  learn new skills 130
  network 124, 127
  personal responsibility 123
  Reduction in Force (RIF) 128
  résumé 123, 126–127
  support group 124
Goal Setting 41, 147–148, 159–160,
    166, 170, 175–177
  finding a new job 123–124

H

Habitat for Humanity 19
Hippocrates 25
Holiday Party 19
Holmes, Marcia 74
Humor 53, 96

I

Illusions. See Bach, Richard
Internships 20

J

Jaworski, Joseph 164
Job Description

job audit 21
Job Satisfaction 60–62, 171

K

Kennedy, John F. 30

L

Leadership 160, 164–165
Listening Skills 50, 102–103, 105–106,
    154, 160, 169, 175
Literacy 147

M

Management by Objective (MBO) 155
Managers. *See* Bosses
McGregor, Douglas 158
Mental Illness and Addictions 142–144.
    See also Addiction; *See also* Depres-
    sion
Mentors 150, 177–178
Merril-Reid Social Styles 25
"Me" File 22
  "Me Résumé." 23
Mission Statement 22, 68, 148–149
Motivating Employees 163–171
  by example 169
  constructive criticism 167
  delegate 166
  desire 164
  differences 166
  fear 163, 167
  goal-setting 166
  leadership 164–165
  listening skills 169
  manage expectations 169
  personality type 166
  praise 169
  respect input 166
  rewards 164, 167–169
  trust 166
Motivating Managers 169–171
  attitude 170
  goal-setting 170
  staying informed 170

Mutual Assessment 155

O

Office politics 63

P

Performance Evaluations 41, 139,
    152–162
  attitude 153
  Behavior Anchored Rating Scales
    (BARS) 154
  communication 153–154, 156–158,
    161
  Critical Incidents Log 155
  developmental 159
  empowerment 153
  expectations 156
  Finding a "Perfect Ten" 155
  growth on the job 161
  listening skills 154, 160
  Management by Objective (MBO) 155
  Mutual Assessment 155
  negative review 160–161
  on-going review 154
  partnership model 159
  personality type 153
  problem solving 161
  productivity 161
  quarterly evaluations 154
  Self-assessment 155
  self-evaluation 154
  support 162
  training 162
  Trait System 154
  "two-against-one" scenario 162
Performax Systems International, Inc. 25
Personality Clash 136–137
Personality Test 33–35
Personality Types 25–35, 44–47, 52–53,
    60–64, 85–87, 90–91, 102,
    136–137, 153, 166
  combinations 30
  command-person 27
  detail-person 27–28
  masking 32

people-person 26–27
personality test 33–35
romance 30
support-person 28–29
working against 31
Personal Life
  attitude 174
  balance personal life and work 173
  emotional involvement 179
  goal-setting 175, 176
  good health 178, 179
  journal 175
  listening skills 175
  mentors 177
  society, interacting with 178
  spiritual 180
Physically Challenged. *See* Disabilities
Policies and Procedures Manual 139
Praise 53, 169
Probationary Warnings 140
Punishment 41, 167

Q

Quitting 109
  analyze your current Job 110
  evaluate options 112
  leave positively 117
  reasons to quit 114
  start your own business 117
  ways not to quit 116

R

Reduction in Force (RIF) 128
Respect 51
Résumé 123, 126–127
  "me" file 23
Rewards 41, 164, 167–169
Rust, Dr. Rene 180

S

Seinfeld, Jerry 29, 30
Self-esteem 71, 144
  affects job 74
  building 72–73, 76–81

co-dependency 78
criticism 79, 101
distorted self-image 71
emotional masks 76
formation 71
good health 77
low self-esteem 74–76
self-image 70
stress and 74
think / thank list 80
work identity 73
your potential 80
Serenity Prayer 92
Seven-year-itch 9
Small businesses 60–63
communication 62
entrepreneurs 61
flexibility 61, 62
job satisfaction 60
personality type 61
Special project 16
Starting your own business 117
Stress 82, 141–142
attitude 95
balance personal life and work 95
burn-out 93
company culture 91
cumulative 86
delegate 96
depression 93–94
emotional control 89
humor 96
level of 85
manage expectations 95
medical expenses 82
on-the-job abuse 108
personality type 85–87, 90–91
physical condition 85, 87, 88, 89
procrastination 96
productivity 82
relieving 94
self-care training 83
stress management programs 83
work environment 141–142
Supervisor. *See* Bosses
Surveys, Employee 149

T

Team 49, 53, 56
building and empowerment 147–148
member termination, impact 140
mentors 150
Trait System 154
Trust 56, 150, 166, 170

V

Values 66–68
Volunteer 19–20

W

Winfrey, Oprah 72
Workaholics 65–67

Z

Ziglar, Zig 177